AL BROWN & STEVE LOGAN
HUNGER
FOR THE WILD

RANDOM HOUSE
NEW ZEALAND

A catalogue record for this book is available from the National Library of New Zealand

A RANDOM HOUSE BOOK
published by
Random House New Zealand
18 Poland Road, Glenfield, Auckland, New Zealand

www.randomhouse.co.nz

First published 2007. Reprinted 2007 (twice), 2008 (four times), 2010

© 2007 Fisheye Films Ltd

The moral rights of the author have been asserted

ISBN 978 1 86941 937 0

Design: Gary Stewart, Ocean Design
Layout: Amy Tansell/Words Alive
Printed in China

CONTENTS

Auckland

Kawhia

Rotorua

Whanganui River

Wanganui

Kapiti Island

Waikanae

Castlepoint

Masterton

Mokihinui River

Picton

Westport

Blenheim

Wellington

Punakaiki

Greymouth

Christchurch

Lyttelton

Birdlings Flat

Queenstown

Cromwell

Bannockburn

Dunedin

INTRODUCTION

Steve Logan and Al Brown share a love of fishing, hunting and the great outdoors. They also run one of the country's most successful fine dining restaurants, Logan Brown Restaurant & Bar in Wellington. In *Hunger for the Wild* they leave the comfort of their restaurant and head to the far corners of the country, meeting up with colourful Kiwi characters to chase down our freshest and finest foods.

It's an exhilarating hunting and culinary journey inspired by the characters, places and food from their award-winning television series. In the book Al and Steve reveal personal insights from these hunting and gathering adventures, sharing stories and photos of the people they met along the way. You'll also find detailed recipes for Al's delicious dishes; Steve's recommended wine matches, as well as useful tips on how to deal with a range of seafood and meat.

The first television series *Hunger for the Wild* was produced by Peter Young and Tracy Roe from Fisheye Films and won *Best Factual Series* at the 2007 Air New Zealand Screen Awards. A second series screened in late 2007.

THOUGHTS FROM STEVE AND AL

For us the highlight of making *Hunger for the Wild* was meeting the wonderful, humble Kiwi characters who shared their lives with us and welcomed us into their part of Aotearoa.

The anticipation of the catch is a common theme for all people who hunt and gather. Mixed with the feeling of excitement and nervousness, it's what drives you – the possibility of gathering the product and the sense of relief when you do, whether it's landing a fish, finding a bed of cockles, or discovering a patch of mushrooms. It's a great feeling to then cook it, give it away or share it with friends and family. There's also the self indulgent re-capping of the story to anyone who cares to listen.

Throughout the *Hunger for the Wild* series we met and spent time with many Maori people. The more we delved, the more we came to understand the incredible connection they have to their land and to their people. Like most New Zealanders, the haka raises the hairs on our necks, but that's just a tiny part of the culture. The time we spent with people like Baldy Haitana up the Whanganui River, Matai Broughton at Castlepoint, Davis Apiti at Kawhia, Nev and Trev Tahuaroa in the Marlborough Sounds, has given us a huge amount of respect for the Maori culture.

On our travels we also reaffirmed that there's still food to be gathered in the wild or on the sides of roads all around New Zealand. People who love food can observe and stumble upon mint, parsley, blackberries, mushrooms, puha, fennel, rosemary and wild thyme and a myriad of other great ingredients.

CRAYFISH ON THE RUGGED WEST COAST

NO NAMBY PAMBY RESORTS HERE

We would have felt a bit cheated if it hadn't been raining as we journeyed on to the West Coast. It seemed like the Holden was the only car on the road, as we edged our way along State Highway 6 through driving rain towards our mate Ginge's remote bach near Punakaiki.

Once we got there, we were lucky enough to experience Ginge's unorthodox and hair-raising way of catching a crayfish for the table, and to explore a remote and rugged region with a heap of colourful characters.

Hidden from the road, with the sky pitch-black and the wind thrashing the wet bush, we did well to find the small track that led to Ginge's place.

It was remote and kind of creepy, so to be welcomed by Ginge's big, smiley, friendly face was a relief. His classic Kiwi bach with its raging fire was a welcome haven from the ominous backdrop of mountain ranges, and the wild expanse of the Tasman Sea before us.

Time seems to have stood still in this part of the world. The huge granite faces behind the bach were covered with bush, mist and waterfalls and the place had an almost prehistoric feel — the sort of place you'd expect to see dinosaurs.

Al: There's a sense of life being a bit on the edge here and that in the West Coast things don't come easy. As a coast that is constantly bombarded with extreme weather and massive ocean seas, you can almost feel the struggle the people who've lived here have endured over the years.

OUR MATE GINGE

Ginge (Tony) Connors looks like a friendly Grizz Wiley — he's a big ginger walrus of a man. With a face full of laughter and a can-do attitude, he's a typical West Coaster. He has been a goldminer, a farmer, secretary of the local Kumara Racing Club, has a number of whitebaiting stands and is a hands-on

Steve: Isolated from the rest of New Zealand by the Southern Alps, Coasters have developed a culture rich in the pioneering values of self-reliance and hospitality.

dad. Ginge's wife Bev is also a 100 per cent West Coaster and a lawyer by day. We met Ginge and Bev about five or six years ago on a trip to the Coast looking for a regular supply of turbot for our restaurant, Logan Brown.

We spent a day meeting local fishermen and later that evening they took us around to have dinner at Ginge and Bev's place. It was your classic West Coast ambush. Here were these two Flash Harrys with a fancy restaurant in Wellington and, without a doubt, Ginge and his mates were thinking 'let's put these guys to task and see what they can do'.

With plenty of ribbing being directed our way we were escorted out the back to a large, old West Coast kitchen. We were presented with a number of different species of fish like cod, turbot and, from memory, there was even some whitebait.

We made a few dishes as quickly as possible as we were dying to join in on a few drinks. We sat around a huge dinner table with a whole lot of Coasters in what was to be an extraordinary evening of laughter, good food and plenty of wine to wash it down.

Driving back to Westport the next day, we stopped off to check out Ginge and Bev's bach and we were blown away by its position on the beautiful, remote coast at Punakaiki. In typical West Coast manner, Ginge showed us where the keys were left and, in his modest fashion, said to use it any time.

SNATCH-POTTING WITH GINGE

Steve: I found it amazing that with a simple rope and net you can catch one of the kings of the seafood species. Sure, it took energy, ingenuity and crazy courage, but the thrill of snatching from the wild is incredible. I'll never forget my morning with Ginge.

Ginge is an expert fisherman and has been catching crays off the rocks near his bach for over 20 years. It's called snatch-potting and is something of a tradition in this neck of the woods, where people have been doing it for generations. As we were to find out, it's one hell of a way to catch a cray!

After winning the toss, it was Steve who had to get up pre-dawn in order to hit the low tide at one of Ginge's favourite spots. Al had the sleep-in but was charged with making some basil mayonnaise and gathering the other ingredients for dinner.

It was a drizzly morning that Steve and Ginge headed out into. The storm had passed but there was a big sea running. Ginge didn't like the look of it but was prepared to give it a go. Ginge reckoned he and Steve were in for a bit of a walk, which in West Coast language means one hell of an adventure.

The adventure began with a steep descent down a bushy track and a walk along a stunning beach, followed by a wade through the sea, a meeting with some grumpy seals and finally a gut-busting scramble up a slippery, sheer cliff.

Once at the top, it was just a matter of dodging birds, avoiding thorny scrub and traversing some treacherous rock crevasses. It turned out that Ginge's spot was a slippery downward-sloping rocky ledge with a sheer 50 foot drop down to a wild, thrashing sea.

'With that below and the grey dawn sky, drizzle and squalling birds pressing in on me from above, it was exciting, exhilarating and petrifying all at once,' Steve recalled.

Bev: It's about terror. I think of him in the early morning pulling on a narrow ledge — often it's quite slippery. He's sure-footed and, rationally, I'm confident he can do it, but there's always a fear in the back of my mind.

CRAYFISH

New Zealand spiny rock lobsters, commonly known as crayfish, are found throughout New Zealand, most often in groups hiding in crevices, rocky ledges and around reefs.

They can live until up to 30 years but reach minimum legal catch size at seven or eight years.

The catch size of spiny rock lobsters is measured by tail width. Females, identified by an extra pair of small pincers on the rear pair of legs, must have a tail width of 60 mm or more to be taken. Males must have a tail width of 54 mm or more.

There is a limit of no more than six rock lobsters per person per day.

New Zealand also has the largest lobster in the world — the packhorse lobster, which is found only in areas north of Mahia Peninsula. To be taken, the packhorse lobster must have a tail length of more than 216 mm.

There are smaller freshwater crayfish called koura found in many parts of New Zealand.

The swell was running high and after a quick survey from his precarious perch, Ginge said that he didn't like their chances. Since they'd come all this way though they weren't going back without giving it a crack. With the tide pushing in there was time for about three decent throws with the snatch pot.

The actual process of snatch-potting is comparatively simple. Ginge ties a fish head to a weighted snatch pot which is like a big basketball hoop but with the net closed off at the bottom. It is tied to a long line of rope secured to the bank where we stood. Ginge throws the snatch pot down into the water below. The art is getting it in the right spot and, once there, he'll leave it for about ten minutes — enough time for the crayfish to be lured onto the net, but not so long that they finish eating and make a quick exit.

Crayfish, or more correctly rock lobsters, usually hang out under rocky ledges, hiding in underwater dens during the day to shelter from predators and storms, but they can also wander large distances across the seafloor. There's strong evidence that they possess a magnetic directional compass and geographic positioning capabilities; however, it's their sense of smell that fishermen rely on to lure crayfish into their traps.

Steve: The craziest thing was that Ginge was oblivious to the risks he was taking. Every time he stepped out onto the ledge I was wondering: What if he went over? What could I do? What would I do? It was probably Ginge's nonchalance, backed up by his years of experience that kept my gob shut. Oh yeah, and the fact that we needed a cray for the cook-up back at the bach!

PULLING THE POT

The critical part of snatch-potting is the actual snatch. Before you do this you have to gently pull up the slack until the rope becomes taut against the pot, the idea is that you don't disturb the crays feeding on the bait. When you have a taut rope you 'snatch' the pot, pulling it quickly and smoothly back up to the surface, keeping the rope tight to prevent the crays from escaping. It's an art that Ginge has perfected, but that day it wasn't getting results. After two throws, all they came up with was a couple of paddle crabs. That's hardly a feed for four, but the thought of returning empty-handed was all the motivation Ginge and Steve needed.

The seas were building as tide and time were working against them. There was just time for one last throw and they were hoping it would be a good one.

GOD SAVE OUR KIWI BACH

Back at the bach Al was enjoying the luxury of a leisurely rise, a cup of fresh coffee and a chance to explore this classic Kiwi bach.

As soon as we walked into Ginge's place there was the immediate feeling

pat and al in blackball

cray dinner

al and bev collecting watercress

ginge

that it had been there forever and had endured everything the Coast could throw at it, weathering the harshest elements throughout the years.

For most New Zealanders the bach or holiday home remains a true Kiwi icon, with a sentimental attachment that has lasted for generations of New Zealanders.

The word 'bach' is literally taken from the word 'bachelor' referring to a man who, perhaps, lived alone in basic surroundings with just the fundamentals required for living. In the south of the South Island a bach is more commonly known as a crib. Most start out as a bit of a lean-to and then over the years another room or window might be added, or a deck, to catch the last of the evening sun. They tend to grow almost organically.

Entering a real bach is like stepping into a time warp — memories of a familiar smell, the single decent chair that everyone fights over, or, perhaps, a particular creaky floorboard. Each bach has its tiny idiosyncrasies that make it unique. People have big ideas about fixing up their baches, but then they're on holiday so rarely get around to it!

BLACK MUSSELS AND SALAMI

Al: The thing I love about cooking in baches is that they've each got a unique personality — there's always an interesting assortment of dishes and bowls that have come and been left over the years, and it's kind of like each little piece has a story. They're always happy places because people are relaxed and on holiday.

Al was unaware of Steve's plight out on the clifftop with Ginge. Meanwhile he'd found a great rocky area not far from the bach that was coated in black mussels and he'd gathered a small sackful. Small black mussels grow abundantly in the rocky tidal zones along the West Coast and are a ready source of seafood for all to gather and enjoy. Smaller than the more commonly eaten greenshell mussels, black mussels are sweet and juicy and the beauty is that you can still get a feed at low tide even if the weather's no good for getting out in the boat. To go with the mussels and crayfish he wanted chorizo — a type of spicy smoked sausage — and he knew exactly where to find some.

Historic Blackball, tucked away on the inland side of the Paparoa ranges, is famous for being the birthplace of the Labour Party. More importantly, its butcher Pat Kennedy — who has been butchering in Blackball since he was 14 years old — is well known up and down the country for making great sausages and salami.

'Having eaten a heap of Pat's products over the years, going into his butcher shop was like visiting the Holy Grail of salami,' said Al. 'It was the first time I had met Pat and it's always great to get to know the person behind a product.'

The remarkable thing about Blackball is that it's basically an old mining town in the middle of nowhere that has rebuilt itself largely around its hotel, Formerly The Blackball Hilton, and Pat's butchery.

It's wonderful to find these great products in such a remote location. You could put that down to the West Coast can-do attitude and willingness to adapt. Pat Kennedy put his head down and worked at what he was good at and the market came to him instead of him going to the market.

Pat gave Al a dozen beautiful chorizo sausages straight from the smoker.

AL'S BASIC BACH MAYO

Everyone should know how to make a real mayo. You can buy other relishes and condiments for the bach, but a good basic mayonnaise makes a huge difference to the way things taste; and compared with a processed supermarket version — well, there's no comparison.

I like a little bit of sugar in there just because I like the balance of sweet and sour and a little bit of heat from the mustard to round out the flavours.

Make a big batch of mayo at the beginning of the holiday and adapt small portions of it, with the addition of one or more ingredients, to suit the dish of the day.

Store the basic mix in an airtight container in the fridge.

INGREDIENTS
4 egg yolks
½ tablespoon dijon mustard
1 lemon (juice of)
1 tablespoon cider vinegar
2 teaspoons sugar
¾ cup olive oil
¾ cup canola or other cooking oil
salt and freshly ground pepper to season

METHOD
Using either a hand-held food blender or food processor fitted with a metal blade, place the egg yolks, mustard, lemon juice, cider vinegar and sugar in the bowl and process for five seconds until incorporated. With the motor running, slowly drizzle in the blended olive and canola oils. Season with salt and pepper.

VARIATIONS
- Add a handful of chopped mint to the mayo and blend for a great accompaniment for things like new potatoes or barbecued lamb.
- Roasted garlic and finely chopped thyme added to the mayo is great with game.
- Add gherkins, red onion, capsicum, grain mustard and capers to make a tartare sauce.
- The addition of bloomed saffron to the mayo is terrific with steamed shellfish.
- Add orange and lemon juice to turn the mayo into a runny citrus sauce.
- Add ground cumin, curry powder and cayenne pepper for an Indian-style mayo that tastes great with marinated chargrilled meats and chicken.

THE FINAL SNATCH

The anticipation was unreal as Ginge stepped out onto the ledge to pull the snatch pot for the third and final time. From where he was sitting Steve couldn't see the pot coming out of the water, all he could hear was Ginge's joyful chuckle as he declared, 'Yay hey, we're in business, Logie!'

What made it even sweeter was that there were three good-sized crays on board — all keepers.

Ginge, never one to miss an opportunity said, 'Righto then, we'll go back and see if they've got some mates!' With one more quick snatch Ginge got another beauty. Four crays and it was time to catch up with Al.

As Ginge and Steve made their long, cold, wet trip home, it was made easier as they anticipated all the glory in arriving with the catch, the big hot and hearty meal to come and the chance to relive tales of the hunt over a few drinks with Al and Bev.

WATERCRESS SALAD

The simplicity of this salad, pure as you like, is hard to beat. It could be made with rocket, watercress, or even a chunk of iceberg lettuce — just keep in mind that it's all about balancing the richness of the other components of the meal.

Simply rinse some watercress, then dress with a drizzle of olive oil, a squeeze of lemon juice and a pinch of salt and pepper.

ROADSIDE DELI

While Steve and Ginge were making their way back, Bev had joined Al back at the bach. She helped clean the mussels and told Al that Ginge had taken her out snatch-potting when they were courting, but that she hadn't been back since.

After cleaning the mussels Bev took Al to a classic West Coast roadside deli, a ditch by the side of the road. It was on prime waterfront, spring-fed real estate — the perfect place to find salad ingredients to go with the crayfish.

To hunt, gather, catch, or harvest from the wild stirs a huge passion in people. From earliest times when hunting and gathering was a means of staving off death until today, each outing into the wild is bound by a common theme — anticipation. There's always an air of excitement, often coupled with a hint of nervousness as one heads out to sea or into the hills, or walks up a stream quietly stalking prey. It's that anticipation that keeps us heading back into the wild. Then there's the point when that anticipation can turn to ecstasy, sheer joy or, in many cases, huge relief as the moment of capture is realised. There is a massive weight that literally falls from your shoulders, which in our case is immediately replaced with a completely different form of anticipation — hunger!

A SHORT HISTORY OF THIS REGION

Population: 31,000.

Main towns are Westport, Hokitika and Greymouth.

Maori came to seek pounamu, the sacred greenstone or nephrite jade.

Gold fever attracted Europeans to the region in the 1860s. In 1866–67 the gold boomtown of Brighton (today Tiromoana) sprang up — within five weeks there were 160 buildings and 53 hotels to support the growing influx of hopeful goldminers.

In the early 1900s the main resource was coal, which was mined on the Coast and delivered to Wellington by ship.

Many colourful characters embraced the isolation. One was farmer Andrew Hunter, who, in the 1930s, designed a huge wooden flume to transport his coal 3 km to Seal Island which offered shelter to the boats that shipped it on to Wellington. Hunter built the flume by hand with suspended ladders, one section at a time. It's long gone now, but his innovative spirit lives on.

The isolated, dangerous coastline has no real harbour. River mouths provide sanctuary, but the crossings were often difficult and dangerous. Shipwrecks and drownings were common in the late nineteenth and early twentieth centuries.

Seafood was always in constant supply and a great natural food source for Maori and European alike. Today fishing remains one of the main economic drivers of this region — Talleys is the largest local employer. Tourism has also grown to be a major source of employment.

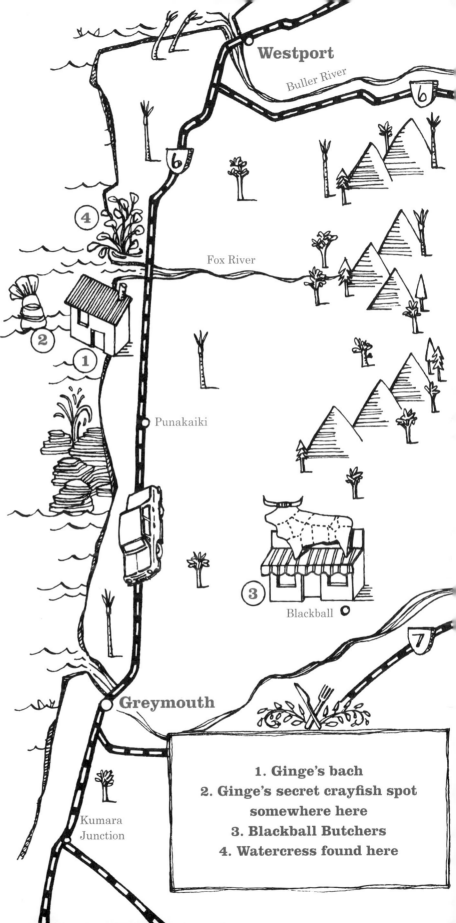

Westport

Buller River

Fox River

Punakaiki

Blackball

Greymouth

Kumara Junction

1. Ginge's bach
2. Ginge's secret crayfish spot somewhere here
3. Blackball Butchers
4. Watercress found here

BARBECUED CRAYFISH WITH MUSSEL & CHORIZO RAGOÛT & BASIL MAYO By Al Brown

This is a great dish that tastes even better when you've gathered the ingredients yourself. However, if you aren't lucky enough to have scored a crayfish, no worries — the chorizo and mussel combination makes for a satisfying dish with or without it. You could easily throw a piece of blue cod on top or, if there are no mussels, use cockles. Don't limit yourself to exactly what's in the recipe.

A crusty hunk of bread and a salad with this completes this meal perfectly. The basil mayo is a variation on Al's basic bach mayo, see page 19. Serves 8 as a main.

STEP 1. BASIL MAYO

INGREDIENTS
1 handful fresh basil leaves
1 cup Al's basic bach mayo
salt and freshly ground black pepper to taste

METHOD
Using either a hand-held blender or food processor fitted with a metal blade, process fresh basil leaves until smooth. Fold the basil mix into the mayo and season with salt and freshly ground black pepper. Refrigerate until required.

STEP 2. CHORIZO RAGOÛT

INGREDIENTS
¼ cup olive oil
350 g chorizo sausage, finely diced
500 g onion, finely diced
250 g celery, finely diced
1 tablespoon garlic, minced
60 g tomato paste
4 cups whole peeled tomatoes, puréed
1 teaspoon sugar

METHOD
Take a large saucepan and place over heat. Once hot add the olive oil and chorizo. Cook for 5 minutes then add the onion, celery and garlic. Turn

down the heat and sweat the vegetables and chorizo for 15 minutes, stirring occasionally. As the water evaporates out of the celery and onions, the flavours will intensify. Finally add the tomato paste, the puréed tomatoes and sugar. Cook for another 15 minutes. Remove from the heat and hold until required. Refrigerate if using the next day.

STEP 3. BLACK MUSSELS STEAMED IN RAGOÛT

INGREDIENTS
3 kg fresh mussels, cleaned and debearded
2 cups white wine
4 crayfish, halved down the centre, cleaned and dried
melted butter
salt and pepper to season
½ cup fresh basil leaves, roughly chopped
2 cups chopped tomatoes
50 g butter, roughly chopped

METHOD
First heat up your barbecue until it's good and hot. Now place a large saucepan on high heat and add the chorizo ragout. Once the ragout is heated through, add the fresh mussels and white wine. Place a lid on the saucepan and turn the heat down to medium.

While the mussels are cooking, brush the crayfish halves with butter or oil then season with salt and pepper. Place the crayfish halves, flesh side down on the grill or flat top and cook for 4 to 5 minutes before turning.

Now check the mussels. They should have started to open up, so add the fresh basil, chopped tomato and butter. Place the lid back on and turn the heat down to low.

The crayfish are ready when the shell has turned bright red and the tail flesh comes away from the cavity with ease.

STEP 4. PLATING AND SERVING

lemon wedges to garnish
crusty bread
watercress salad

To serve, divide the mussels into 8 bowls and spoon over liberal amounts of the chorizo ragoût. Take the tails of the crayfish, remove the flesh from the shell cavities and slice into pieces. Place on top of the steaming hot mussels. Finish with a dollop of basil mayo and garnish with a lemon wedge. Serve with heaps of crusty bread for dipping, and watercress salad on the side.

STEVE'S TIPS ON HOW TO PREPARE AND BARBECUE CRAYFISH

- Split the crayfish in two, starting with the crayfish on its back, cutting from the mouth down through the centre of the body using a combination of slicing and chopping actions.

- Pull out and wash the innards or any parts you don't want to eat.

- To ensure a nice seal when the cray hits the hot plate dry the flesh with paper towels.

- Brush with butter or oil and sprinkle with salt and pepper.

- Ensure the barbecue is hot enough — the crayfish should sizzle from the moment it hits the plate.

- Place the crayfish flesh-side down first for 4 to 5 minutes. Turn and finish off cooking on the shell side for 3 to 4 minutes.

- If your barbecue has a lid, close it to speed things up and generate all-round heat. If not, cover the crayfish with a roasting pan to achieve the same effect.

- It pays to err on the side of undercooking crayfish as it will continue to cook after it comes off the barbecue.

STEVE'S WINE RECOMMENDATION

Neudorf Chardonnay from Nelson
Wherever we travel we gather food from the region so we try to incorporate wine from local vineyards, too. Neudorf is a fabulous producer of elegant yet full-flavoured and well-structured wines, especially Chardonnay. Their Chardonnay has weight and power that stands up well to the rich and robust mussel stew. Its fresh, citrus character complements the crayfish and creamy basil mayonnaise, freshening the palate after every sip.

WILD PIGS UP THE WHANGANUI RIVER

TELLING PORKIES

'So do you eat wild food very often?' we asked local Whanganui River pig-hunting legend Baldy Haitana.

'Whaddya mean?' he replied, looking at us as if we were from another planet! 'It's all we eat! If it's not wild boar, then it's wild venison, eel or trout.' It was a poignant reminder that some people still hunt and gather nearly all their food.

We were heading into the remote reaches of the Whanganui River to chase down some wild pork for Al's braised pork belly dish. Along the way, we heard stories of life on the river and tall tales of hunting escapades, while getting to grips with the real guts of hunting and gathering.

We'd been serving wild boar at Logan Brown every winter since we opened in 1996 and our wild boar pie is considered one of our signature dishes. Wild boar arrives at our restaurant by courier, hygienically vacuum sealed in a poly bin, so it was time to take a step closer to the source!

Al: My first experience eating wild boar was in a truck stop on the Napier–Taupo road where they sold roasted wild boar sammies with apple sauce. It sure beat Mum's Marmite and lettuce!

JOURNEYING UP THE WHANGANUI RIVER

Steve won the toss on this trip and, after a couple of hours driving on what must be one of New Zealand's narrowest and windiest roads, Al dropped him off at Pipiriki at the end of the Whanganui River road. There he was met by pig-hunting partners Baldy Haitana and Moon Munro.

'Waiting beside the river to be picked up, I was a bit apprehensive,' recalled Steve. 'I'd heard pig hunters were hard men and here I was, pretty much a soft restaurateur who'd never been pig hunting, wondering what the hell I was getting myself into.'

When these two big guys in bush shirts finally made an entrance in their grunty jet boat with a big rooster tail, apprehension turned into raw excitement.

To follow was an hour's trip up river in Moon's jet boat and then a 45-minute slog up to one of Baldy's favourite hunting grounds, Tangahoe, a once-abandoned dairy farm now owned by their friend Dave Davey.

'After brief introductions to Baldy, Moon, and their dogs, Mouse, Bud and Chief, I climbed aboard, found a seat amongst the chaos of packs, rifles and dogs and then we were off.'

The river was spectacular. Speeding across the sparkling green water, through fine mist and the occasional rapid, the high cliffs with native bush reaching down to the river create a sense of eeriness as if they still contain the secrets of battles fought through the years over this hugely important river.

'On the journey up the river I first got a sense of how important and special the Whanganui is to Baldy. For hundreds of years it has been the main highway and the life blood of his people,' said Steve.

Baldy, of Te Atihau-Nui-A-Paparangi, one of the three main tribes along the river, had been selected by his elders to pass on knowledge and stories through to the next generation. He told Steve how he was presented to one of his elders who started telling him all about his ancestors and their history.

During the boat trip Baldy shared the stories and history of his iwi and a proverb which they use wherever they go in New Zealand.

E rere mai te awanui
mai i te kahuimaunga ki Tangaroa
Ko au te awa ko te awa ko au

From the mountain to the sea
flows this mighty river
I am the river and the river is me

A short distance up river Baldy pointed out the pole holes that, over hundreds of years, had been worn into the river banks by his people as they poled their canoes up and down the river.

It was an honour to be invited to travel up the river by Baldy — it would have certainly been seen as a privilege in the old days when there was no right of passage. When Steve asked him if, in the old days, people paid to travel along the river, he replied, 'Pay? I don't know about that. They might have had to pay with their life.'

It was a short stint in the jet boat to Tangahoe landing but there was still a long hard slog up a steep hill between them and some prime pig country.

WHANGANUI RIVER TRADERS' MARKET

While Steve was on the hunt, Al headed to the Whanganui River Traders' market to find something to serve with the pork. This vibrant Saturday market was set up on a site where Whanganui Maori traded with early Europeans.

'To me this was what a market should be. There was a blend of not only edible products but also a lot of arts and crafts — from the Sisters of Compassion selling their preserves next to the woman weaving flax hats, to the white elephant stalls, where an old guy was selling a weathered pair of flippers for five bucks, a possum skin, a small bowl of black boy peaches from his tree. He had a colourful collection of just about everything,' said Al.

Al picked up kumara and corn for the mash and at the stand met local livewire and one of the founders of the market, Annette Main. Annette sells wonderful kumara bread at the market, but to Al's disappointment, it had sold out. She suggested he call in at her house on his way back to Tangahoe.

BAKING BREAD AT THE FLYING FOX RETREAT

Al decided to take up the offer of some kumara bread. Annette owns the Flying Fox Retreat, which offers accommodation to travellers in the region.

Located miles up the Whanganui River on the opposite side of the river from the road, The Flying Fox is accessible only by aerial cable or river boat. The aerial cable, designed and built by her husband John Blythe, is an amazing way to get across a river, especially in such a remote and tranquil place. It's like entering another world — there's a sense of arrival, and the feeling of having stepped out of the rat race for a while is slightly intoxicating.

Annette's an incredibly busy person, dividing her time between running The Flying Fox, duties as deputy chair on the regional council, growing vegetables and baking bread for the weekly market. Yet, for all that busyness, she has a great, unhurried warmth about her.

Annette and John are both very creative and there's a sense that they've made a little piece of their own world, just the way they want it. The cottages are built and decorated with a grown-up hippy feel about them. They're adorned with local art, showers overlooking the river, composting toilets — even the barbecue we cooked on that evening is a work of art.

Annette is especially proud of her heritage apple trees, survivors of times past when the people at nearby Koroniti Marae used these sunny flats above the river to grow fruit and vegetables.

Annette's kumara bread was outstanding. 'There's something really special about someone who makes bread. It's like they're born with the "dough gene". It takes patience and a certain feel. I've got none of that. I don't have patience for a start. I'm very good at cooking things quickly on high heat, but making bread by hand is a time-consuming passion. It tends to be people like Annette who are deliberate, unfazed and somehow have a lovely aura and flow to their lives, who seem to make the best breads.'

FLYING FOX KUMARA BREAD

This bread has that delicious, distinctive, homemade taste. It's not a light, airy bread — it's slightly sweet, with a little bit of a yeasty flavour and a gorgeous colour due to the orange kumara used in the recipe. It's the sort of bread that makes you want to sit down with a lump of butter and demolish the whole loaf.

Annette adapted this from a recipe by internationally renowned chef Peter Gordon, who is Wanganui born and bred and now runs several highly successful eateries, including Providores and the Tapa Room in London and Dine and Bellota in Auckland. She makes this bread with locally sourced organic orange kumara.

Makes 1 standard loaf.

INGREDIENTS
500 g orange kumara, or any other kumara variety, peeled and chopped
400 ml milk
3 teaspoons yeast
50 ml warm water
750 g flour, preferably organic
1½ teaspoons salt
1 tablespoon olive oil

METHOD
Boil the orange kumara in the milk until liquid is reduced by half. Cool to room temperature then mix in yeast previously softened in the warm water. Mix in flour, salt, and olive oil and knead until smooth, approximately 10 minutes.

Leave to prove in a warm place until doubled in size. Knead again briefly and form into loaves. Leave to rise again and bake at 350°C for approximately 30 minutes.

HUNTING DOGS

Steve, Moon and Baldy arrived at Tangahoe, a few hundred acres of pasture surrounded by bush, on a plateau above the Whanganui River. Always marginal for farming, it has twice been abandoned and was a perfect place for their pig hunt.

On the walk up Steve learnt a bit more about pig hunting and pig hunters. Moon and Baldy are among this unique breed of Kiwi that love marching through the bush for hours on end with nothing more than their dogs, guns and the chance to chase down a wild pig. It's a form of hunting that usually involves a lot of walking, followed by a quick chase and hands-on combat as the hunter wrestles the pig into position so that he can 'stick' it with a knife, hopefully in the heart so that the pig will quickly bleed to death. It's a primal activity that runs on adrenalin, dirt, blood, sweat and grime. At the end of the day it makes for some great yarns and plenty of laughs. By the time they'd reached the top of the hill they'd had a fair share of both.

Steve found out that Baldy (Paora) Haitana is called Baldy because he has an impressive head of hair whereas Moon (Craig) Munro's nickname reflects his lack of hair.

Moon lives in Raetihi and goes out hunting whenever he can. He has a reputation for having a great team of hunting dogs and being an excellent man in the bush. He'd have to be if Baldy chose him as his hunting partner. On the River, Baldy is considered a legend.

Steve reckoned it was great to watch them both travel through the bush and see how in tune they were with their surroundings — they were always on the look out for a 'sign' and keeping an eye on their dogs, the key for successful pig hunting.

Baldy and Moon's dogs were great companions and worshipped their masters, but it's something that cuts both ways. These guys have a huge respect for their dogs and how they put themselves on the line in the hunt.

'They'll get chewed up today. They get a hiding today then a couple of days later they're ready to go do it for you all over again. You jump in and grab a pig and they'll be right in there with ya, they're loyal, really loyal,' Baldy told Steve.

While pig dogs may look like mongrels, many are bred specifically for different hunting roles, the main ones being baling and holding. The balers nip the back end of the pig whenever it tries to run away. This has the effect of making the pig sit down or back into a corner and face you. The holders go in and grab the ear if the pig tries to run away and they hold on to it. Good dogs work as a team and Steve was looking forward to seeing them in action.

Baldy: This place is not just about pig hunting — there's a lot of history here and a lot of memories of old people who lived and shared this vision.

THE HUNT BEGINS

Steve: I was a little apprehensive about my ability to keep up and contribute to the hunt. As I waited I realised a quick re-read of my war comic collection left me still a little undone . . .

The hunters headed out at dawn. In shorts, bush shirts with a bit of rope tied round their waists, boots, sheath knives, and rifles — everything that was needed for the job at hand.

Pig hunting is definitely more combative than other forms of hunting. When cornered, these pigs will take on anything and anyone. With a set of sharp tusks they can do a lot of damage in a very short time. The thought of that brought an air of anticipation. The dogs were scouting and Moon and Baldy set a good pace through the bush.

Because pigs don't have sweat glands to regulate their temperature, they wallow in water or mud to cool down. It wasn't long before Moon came across a wallow that had been freshly used. The dogs' ears pricked up and they took off searching for scent. Baldy and Moon quickened the pace as they tried to keep up. It's a time to keep on guard.

'There's always a chance they could get killed, you've got to recognise when the dog is onto a sign, a scent, so to break down that element of danger you've got to get to them as quick as you can while they've got the pig,' said Baldy.

As they moved through the bush a silence fell upon them, something dangerous was about to happen — it carried its own sort of energy. It was a time to be on top of things. Baldy and Moon were totally tuned into the hunt and Steve was working hard to keep up.

And then they heard a bark, and that was the signal. One of the dogs had got on to a pig. Instantly it moved from quietly stalking, to an adrenalin-pumping chase.

'We were charging off through the scrub. Moon and Baldy were shouting and cussing, and the barking was getting closer and louder,' recalled Steve. 'Baldy and Moon were a way ahead, there's no track, and I could only follow their sounds as they crashed through the bushes going down deeper and deeper into a gully.

'Just as I caught up, I heard a dog yelp loudly then Baldy shouting to Moon "Shoot it! Shoot it!" . . . a crack of a rifle, then deathly silence. I arrived in time to see Moon sticking a big, ugly, old boar in the heart to finish it off.'

The young dog, Mouse, had gone in when he shouldn't have. Bud had gone in to help and the boar ripped up both of them. Moon had to shoot the boar to save his dogs.

Panting and sweating, everyone crouched around the bloodied pig and watched it in its death throes. The dogs panting, two of them bleeding, were amped from the heat of battle. The smell of the hunt was thick in the air — it's heady stuff.

Then they were all laughing, relieved from the rush of it all. They'd got their pig and that's what they'd come here for. But little did Steve know that the job was only half done.

annette

moon and bud

dave butchering the boar

steve moon and baldy

tucking in at tangahoe

PIGS

Pigs were liberated by Captain Cook in the 1770s and, later, by sealers and early settlers, both to supply Maori with a new domestic animal and to provide stranded voyagers with food on outlying islands.

Pigs were initially welcomed as an excellent food source, but as their population grew they became a pest, ruining crops and killing wildlife.

Feral pigs, known as Captain Cookers, were well established throughout the country by the 1840s. They can be extremely aggressive when cornered. The tusks, which grow on both sexes, are sharp and can cause serious damage.

Pigs are omnivores feeding mostly on ferns, roots and other crops, and fresh or dead meat. They generally prefer to feed during dawn, dusk and at night.

In New Zealand, an adult boar can weigh up to 180 kg and grow up to 80 cm high. Sows are slightly smaller.

DRAGGING UP THE BOAR

With all the excitement of the hunt, Steve had forgotten that they had actually chased the boar down to the bottom of a deep steep gully. There was only one way out and that was up. Baldy had gutted the boar and used twine to tie the legs up, and when that was done he said to Steve, 'Your job next.'

'Baldy and Moon hoisted 80 kg or so of musky, bloodstained pig over my shoulders and the excruciating climb to the top began. My shoes were a bit slick, and my skinny little legs were struggling. I was constantly doing face plants,' recalled Steve.

'We wanna get home before dark, mate,' ribbed Baldy with his usual sense of humour. There's no question that carrying the pig out is the hardest part of the hunt and the sledging continued all the way to the top.

'I was sweating like a pig, literally! What's worse was being cheek to jowl with the boar's blood-stained, floppy head slapping into me with each step.

'After a bit of help, we finally arrived back on the plateau and built a big manuka scrub fire to "muriwai" the pig, which means to singe off the hair and get rid of any ticks and lice. The smoky manuka flavour was an added bonus,' recalled Steve.

No one can say you don't deserve getting a boar on your plate when you've chased it down and dragged it all the way back up a steep slippery hill!

CATCHING UP WITH THE BOYS AT TANGAHOE

After gathering kumara and corn from the market and Annette's kumara bread, it was time for Al to catch up with the boys up at Dave Davey's farm, Tangahoe, to see if they had caught the prize for the main course. Unless you travel along the river, the only way to get there is by small plane.

'I'm not the best in little planes,' says Al. 'This one was older than the Holden! Kelly, the pilot, looked about 12 and I guess I didn't really know if we were going to land on a nice airstrip or something else!'

They took off from National Park, happy that it was a lovely day. Flying over native bush Al could spy one bit of clear land in the middle of it all. After circling the paddock a couple of times to move the sheep, the plane landed on a side of a hill — fortunately, it was the upside!

It's also the only other way to get things out, and Dave uses every opportunity to load up the plane on the return journey. This time it was bales of wool, but many's the time Kelly, the pilot, has shared the plane with live sheep.

Dave Davey was born and bred at Tangahoe. As a young man he hunted pigs, which at that stage infested the farm. It took a concerted hunting effort from the Pig Hunting Club at Raetihi and a dedicated poison campaign to get things back under control. Even today, Dave still relies on recreational hunters like Baldy and Moon to keep pig numbers in check.

Dave built the lodge at Tangahoe in 1984 and occasionally runs hunting trips to help subsidise the farm.

COOKING IN 'THE LODGE'

These days most of us think about a lodge as a five-star affair with crisp winter-white linen, salubrious surroundings and everything served with the utmost decorum.

The 'lodge' at Tangahoe is a bit more basic. It's just one room used as a base for hunting or work on the far reaches of the property.

Sparsely decorated with deer heads, antlers and skins scattered around, there is little evidence of civilisation — no power poles, no farm tracks, nothing but nature, with mountains and bush in all directions.

There's a generator and an old, wood-burning stove. This sort of stove's a challenge, but a whole lot of fun as well, as it tests your skill as a cook and usually humbles you slightly. This is how everyone used to cook, always having to think about the state of the fire and what heat it was radiating. There's no fancy temperature gauge, so it's back to cooking by feel, but still in the end knocking out some good tucker.

When Steve and the hunters returned, Al and Steve set to braising the pork belly in the wood-fired stove.

At the end of the day it was a real pleasure to share the spoils of the hunt with our new mates, the guys who shared their time, skills and experience with us. There's a huge amount of effort in getting a pig from the wild. It's not for the faint-hearted.

Over dinner, we re-lived the thrill of the hunt — there was plenty of friendly ribbing, Baldy's karakia and an incredible feed made all the tastier by the hunger pangs from the effort of hunting and gathering. It's an experience we will never forget.

A SHORT HISTORY OF THIS REGION

Known as the 'Rhine of New Zealand', the Whanganui River is the longest navigable river in the country with more than 200 rapids, each with its own name and story.

The 290-km long river rises on the northern slopes of Mount Tongariro, one of three active volcanoes of the central plateau, and flows through Taumarunui and the King Country before flowing past the small villages of Pipiriki, Jerusalem and Koroniti and, eventually, ending in the tidal estuary on the outskirts of Wanganui.

The river is a taonga, or a special treasure to Maori. It was the home of a large proportion of Maori villages in pre-European days and is of special spiritual importance.

The river used to be full of eels and fish and it became an important trading route for the thousands of people living along the river.

The first Europeans landed at the river mouth in 1831.

Colonel Wakefield visited Wanganui in 1840, buying a huge amount of land which he traded for guns, blankets, shirts and fish hooks. Several years later a further sum of money was also paid. However, the sale was not recognised by many hapu and ownership is still disputed.

Jerusalem, or Hiruharama, was once an important fishing village or kainga on the river where a Roman Catholic mission was established in 1854 by Suzanne Aubert. More commonly known as Mother Mary Joseph, many Catholics believe she may, one day, be anointed New Zealand's first saint, as the order was highly respected for its charitable nursing. Well-known New Zealand poet James K Baxter formed a community at Jerusalem in the 1970s.

Wanganui, population 43,300, was, at one time, the most prosperous and important city in New Zealand. In the 1926 census, it was the largest provincial city in the country with a population of 26,521, but soon after, Wanganui experienced a long period of decline.

Raetihi

Wanganui River

Pipiriki

Jerusalem

Wanganui

1. Tangahoe
2. Moon and Baldy picked Steve up here
3. Flying Fox
4. River traders' market

CIDER BRAISED WILD BOAR BELLY WITH KUMARA CORN MASH & SAUTÉED APPLE By Al Brown

This is a style of food that I absolutely adore. It's winter fare that's big, robust and gutsy. At the same time, it's pretty traditional. Pork with kumara and corn, flavoured with a bit of rosemary, cider and apple, all makes sense. This combination has been done for years and years, not only by New Zealanders, but by people all over the world. Crackling, gravy, apple and pork conjure up memories of good times!

Cooking with wild food and not something off a feed-lot in Hawke's Bay, it's important to choose a cooking method that will break down the toughness of the meat.

The belly in this dish tastes wonderful and slightly sticky — cooking it down by braising concentrates the flavours and the demi-glaze and rosemary make great gravy.

The gutsy style of the dish also matched the personality of the pig hunters we were feeding, who'd been up since the crack of dawn. The only thing those boys wanted us to add were a couple of fried eggs, which we duly did!

Serves 8 as a main.

STEP 1. CIDER BRAISED WILD BOAR BELLY

INGREDIENTS
1.5 kg wild boar belly or farmed pork belly, ribs removed
salt and pepper to season
500 g onion, rough chopped
250 g celery, rough chopped
50 g garlic cloves, rough chopped
2 cups cider, sweeter, rather than dry
1½ cups chicken stock
2 cups beef stock or demi-glaze
$^1/_3$ cup fresh rosemary leaves
50 g butter
50 g flour

METHOD

Heat the oven to about 130°C.

Cut the boar belly into portion-sized pieces. Heat up a skillet, season the belly with salt and pepper and sear on both sides until caramelised. Be careful not to overcrowd the pan as this boils the meat. Place in roasting dish or ovenware dish.

While the skillet is still on the heat, add the onion, celery and garlic. Cook the vegetables for 10 minutes or so, until they begin to colour.

Now pour in the cider and chicken stock, deglaze the skillet and pour it all over the boar belly.

Finish by adding the beef stock, or better still the demi-glaze, and sprinkle over the fresh rosemary leaves. Cover with tinfoil and place in the oven. Check after 2½ hours and then in 30 minute intervals.

The boar belly is ready when it is tender and falls apart with a fork. Once cooked, remove the belly and place in a suitable ovenproof dish. Now strain off the braising liquid and discard the vegetables.

Place another saucepan on the heat and melt the butter, then add the flour. Whisking all the time, pour in the braising liquid and whisk until the sauce thickens. Check the seasoning then pour the sauce over the braised boar belly. Refrigerate until required.

STEP 2. APPLES

INGREDIENTS

3 cooking apples, Granny Smith or similar

METHOD

Place a saucepan half-filled with water on the heat and bring up to a rolling boil. Peel the apples and slice each into 8 pieces, discarding the core. Place in the boiling water for two minutes until slightly soft. Strain off the apple and hold until required.

STEP 3. KUMARA CORN MASH

Kumara is traditionally served with pig, especially with wild pig, which lends itself well to a bit of sweetness. The mix of kumara and corn is sweet, and buttery — it's a beautiful combination of flavour and texture.

INGREDIENTS

1.2 kg golden kumara, peeled
4 whole corn cobs
50 g butter
⅓ cup milk
salt and pepper to taste

METHOD

Place the chopped kumara in a suitable saucepan and cover with cold salted water. Place on high heat and bring up to the boil.

Place another saucepan on the heat with salted water. Once that begins to boil add the four shucked corn cobs. Cook these for 10 minutes then turn off the heat.

Once the kumara is soft, strain off the water, add the butter and milk, and mash until smooth. Now slice the corn kernels from the cobs and fold into the mashed kumara. Add salt and pepper to taste.

STEP 4. PLATING AND SERVING

braised boar belly
kumara and corn mash
cooked apple slices
butter
sauce

Place the boar belly in a hot oven and bring up to heat. Likewise heat up your kumara and corn mash. Place a sauté pan on medium heat and sauté the par-cooked apple slices in butter until golden.

To serve, place a good amount of kumara and corn mash in the centre of each plate. Top the mash with a portion of the braised belly, and then garnish with the sautéed apple pieces and spoon around the extra sauce to finish.

A great accompaniment with this dish would be a large bowl of steamed watercress.

STEVE'S WINE RECOMMENDATION

Millton Gisborne Chenin Blanc

Chenin Blanc is relatively unknown in New Zealand, but in France it's the grape used to make the famous white wine vouvray. Millton, an organic producer, makes one of the best Chenin Blancs in the country. It's got a rich and satisfying structure that measures up to the robust savoury pork. The wine's honey and citrus character complements the dish and its slight sweetness is a good foil for the smoky pork loin rack.

WHITEBAITING ON THE MOKIHINUI RIVER

I COULD DO THIS DAY AFTER DAY

On the West Coast whitebait are not just a seasonal delicacy — they are a currency with a far greater value than the price they fetch on the open market. Whitebait in exchange for a warrant of fitness or fresh produce is a great way to stretch the budget and share this delicacy around.

Al: To be given half a pound of whitebait is probably one of the greatest gifts, you'll never forget it.

Timing our trip to Mokihinui around the whitebait season, which on the West Coast runs from 1 September to 14 November, we were looking forward to indulging in a pound or three of 'West Coast gold' while finding out more about whitebait culture on the Mokihinui River.

Whitebait is incredibly expensive due to its limited season, erratic supply and strong demand — it's right up there with other sought-after delicacies, such as truffles, saffron and Champagne.

Charles Heaphy, who explored the West Coast in the 1880s, observed that the whitebait were so thick, the dogs were licking them out of the water. Times have changed since then and, over the years, as the number of whitebait has decreased, regulations have increased. The first regulations were introduced as far back as the 1890s after people realised the commercial potential of the fishery.

WHITEBAIT COOKING COMPETITION AT THE MOKIHINUI PUB

The West Coast is a long way from most places and, being 30 kilometres north of Westport, the beachside community of Mokihinui is just a bit more isolated than most. With a population of about 40, the hub of this tiny settlement is the local pub, which serves as a drinking hole, community centre and central meeting place.

We thought that a good way to meet a few locals and a few kilos of their whitebait would be to put up a hundred bucks as first prize for a whitebait

cooking competition at the pub. So, a couple of days ahead of our planned arrival, we organised a few posters and started to get the word out.

We were absolutely stoked when we turned up on the Sunday evening. There was a massive turn-out, with probably more than a hundred people, young and old, and a few dogs, too. Some were from out-of-town places like Nelson, Christchurch and Kaikoura, many were staying in caravans in the local camping ground for the whole season. You could feel the enthusiasm and camaraderie that comes from everybody having a common interest — whitebait. It binds them, it divides them, and it's the stuff of legends.

With typical West Coast hospitality, the locals had gone to the trouble of setting up burners and the ladies had brought plates of food. There was wild pork, venison stew and an assortment of Asian dishes, alongside classic Kiwi fare, such as sponge cakes, asparagus rolls and savouries. It was a magical, colourful West Coast scene with a real party atmosphere.

Some people brought their special frying pans; others garnished their dishes with flowers or cut tomatoes and lemons. It was a serious business — more about the honour of winning than the $100.

The entries were many and varied, including whitebait vol-au-vents, a whitebait and goats' cheese omelette, and a few variations on the classic whitebait fritter served with buttered, sliced white bread and a squeeze of lemon. There were some great dishes and some not-so-great dishes. Amongst the latter was one aptly named a 'feed of whitebait', which consisted of a duck egg warmed in a bit of oil with two pounds of partially thawed whitebait thrown in and stirred until hot. Salt and pepper were not welcome!

The big thing for us about food in our restaurant is flavour, so when we were judging we were after something that was cooked perfectly and tasted great, with the right amount of seasoning and a little bit of originality. There were some great dishes and the eventual winner was Maria Cunningham, the owner of the pub with her Quarter Pounder Mokihinui style. Her giant fritter had a very high whitebait to egg ratio. It was beautifully formed, cooked to golden brown in butter and perfectly seasoned with sea salt and lemon — delicious simplicity.

QUARTER POUNDER MOKIHINUI STYLE

INGREDIENTS

¼ lb (125 g) whitebait   salt and pepper to season
1 egg   sea salt
1 generous lump of butter   1 lemon

METHOD

Lightly beat the egg and stir in the whitebait. Season with salt and pepper. Pour into a hot, well-buttered frying pan. Cook the patty until it's golden on each side. Serve with ground sea salt and a very generous squeeze of lemon juice on top. Enjoy with a salad on the side.

In memory of T.O. — A great Coaster,
great whitebaiter and top bloke.

WHITEBAIT AT LOGAN BROWN

As we do with all seasonal seafoods, we celebrate the arrival of whitebait at the start of each season. Being able to order whitebait in the lead-up to Christmas is perfect timing — it's the end of winter, a time of celebration, asparagus is starting to pop through, and strawberries are tasting sweet. There are a whole lot of things around that make people happy.

We've never done whitebait patties or fritters at Logan Brown — we've always felt that by adding egg you lose flavour, and it's such a delicate taste that we like to keep the whitebait as pure and simple as possible.

We've served whitebait lightly floured and quickly sautéed, with fresh asparagus and a beurre blanc sauce, see page 64 and sautéed, served in buttered white bread with just a squeeze of lemon juice and tartare sauce on the side. Either way, it's always popular. People enjoy the simplicity and delicacy of unadulterated whitebait and we sell heaps.

CATCHING THESE TINY FISH

It was time to try our luck at catching a few of these tiny fish. We've served hundreds and hundreds of kilos of whitebait in the restaurant over the years, but rarely have we caught and tasted it straight from the source.

The whitebait-cooking competition was a great way to meet a few local whitebaiting legends and it gave us the break we were looking for. We were invited to join T.O. (Tony) McGrath and Sos (Brian) Morgan who together work one of the best stands on the Mokihinui. It's been in their families since their fathers fished it together over 50 years ago.

Stands are prized possessions on the Coast and the 650 registered whitebait stands spread over 23 rivers in this region, are administered by the West Coast Regional Council based in Greymouth.

There is a two-inch thick book of guidelines and rules around the use of the stands. On top of that, each river has its own set of 'locals' rules' that have been developed over the years.

The Mokihinui River is not only a great place to catch whitebait, it's also incredibly beautiful and home to trout and a myriad of birds, including blue herons, tui, bellbirds, ducks and the odd wood pigeon.

'The whitebait season brings to the fore a huge amount of camaraderie on local rivers, and as much as you hear about the odd stoush, it's a very social thing revolving around the bait running,' said Steve. 'Many people return year after year, creating long-lasting friendships on the banks of the river.'

Being the type of hunting and gathering that attracts both males and females of all ages, the social aspect almost takes over from the fishing. But there's no doubt that it's the 'anticipation gene' that keeps people coming back, armed with stories of yesteryear and high hopes for bumper hauls of whitebait.

They all love to catch and eat whitebait and to have enough left over to give away. The beauty of whitebait is that it doesn't need to be cleaned or gutted — anyone can handle it when given some.

THE WHITEBAIT STAND

Whitebait stands on the West Coast are as unique as the people who built them. Most of the stands have shelters built with plenty of West Coast ingenuity from odd bits of building material, such as old sheets of corrugated iron, timber, tarpaulin and baling twine.

Many stand owners try to make them as comfortable as possible with couches and old car seats and some form of simple cooking facility. Most have jetty-like structures of regulated length, made of metal and wood, built over the river's edge.

The stand we visited typified many in the area — it's really three separate stands, which are fished as one. Sos and T.O. continue their families' tradition, working the stands together and sharing the catch. Along with the usual cobbled-together bits of shelter, Sos's stand also has an old fridge, a sink, a

pulley system for lowering the stand and a great, rusty, old, pot-belly stove, which serves as a heater and something to boil the kettle on for a cuppa or to fry up a few whitebait.

Sos Morgan is a real legend — he's the unofficial mayor of Mokihinui and it seemed like he'd fished the river longer than anyone else. He's a local dairy farmer who milks 120 cows every morning before heading to the river, where he upholds the local whitebaiting etiquette. He has also been a commercial fisherman and worked as a carpenter at Stockton mine for a while. Sometimes, too, he is called upon to be a local caterer — if anyone wants a party they'll usually call Sos to arrange a spit.

Being an experienced whitebaiter, Sos has learned all the signs that the whitebait will be running. 'You can go days without any whitebait, and then the blue herons will turn up — that'll be the day you'll get whitebait,' he told us.

T.O. is also a pretty staunch whitebaiter and told us stories of his father and his mates who, on their best day, scooped over 800 pounds of whitebait out of the river.

Strips of white board, called 'spotters', are lined up across the shallow to the water's edge. It is easy to see the whitebait as they swim over the boards. 'It's incredibly beautiful to see a shoal of whitebait swimming upstream,' said Al. 'We only saw one quarter-of-a-pound shoal but there can be 50-pound shoals and when that happens the excitement is huge — it's probably akin to the feeling goldminers get.'

The rule on the Mokihinui River is that only scoop-netting is allowed from the stands — it's considered to be fairer than using set nets. Set-netting is only allowed further up the river past the registered stands. This rule tends to be the opposite of most other river's rules in the region. Most whitebaiters at the stands don't sell their catch commercially, they tend to either freeze it or give it away.

OLD-FASHIONED HOSPITALITY

While we were at the stand, Sos's mum Fran, who lives just up the road, turned up as she does most days, with a plate full of baking — that day it was sponge drops. The light-as-air miniature sponges were filled with cream and a dot of red jelly and had been dusted with icing sugar. They were perfect.

It was a lovely contrast to sit, surrounded by raw nature, and have someone arrive with a plate of delicate sweet treats. 'It's that act of giving food that's so lovely, and it's something we are losing in New Zealand,' says Al. 'Baking something and taking it round to a friend's place is so much more personal than turning up with a packet of Mallowpuffs. It's a bit like writing a letter instead of sending an email.'

The West Coast seems to have maintained a generous hospitality that's all but disappeared in much of urban New Zealand. It's an old style of living based on self-reliance and giving, where people find the time to keep up these wonderful traditions alive.

FRAN'S SPONGE DROPS

INGREDIENTS
a pinch of salt
3 eggs, separated
³/₄ cup caster sugar
1 dessertspoon plain flour
1 cup cornflour
1 teaspoon baking powder
whipped cream, to serve
red jelly, to serve

METHOD
Preheat the oven to 175°C on fan bake. Add salt to egg whites and beat until soft peaks form. Add sugar gradually one tablespoon at a time, ensuring that the sugar is dissolved. Add egg yolks and beat until well combined. Gently fold in sifted flour, cornflour and baking powder. Using a teaspoon, drop small spoonfuls onto a greased baking tray or tray lined with baking paper.

Bake for 7 to 10 minutes until very light golden. Remove and cool on rack. Sandwich pairs together with whipped cream and a teaspoon of red jelly.

Dust with icing sugar.

sos morgan

pub cook-up

hanging out on the stand

WHITEBAIT

Whitebait is the juvenile form of the Galaxiidae family of native fish. There are five different species that are caught as whitebait on the West Coast.

The juveniles of five species are almost indistinguishable, varying slightly in colour and form and ranging from 45–65 mm in length.

The most common species is inanga (*Galaxias maculatus*), which make up about 80 per cent of the whitebait catch. The next most common is koaro (*G. brevipinnis*), followed by giant kokopu (*G. argenteus*), short-jawed kokopu (*G. postvectis*) and banded kokopu (*G. fasciatus*).

The three species of kokopu are considered to be threatened as numbers decline, probably due to loss of habitat — swampy and shaded streams — and overfishing.

The West Coast whitebait season runs from 1 September to 14 November from early morning to early evening, fishing on the incoming tide. There are strict guidelines on fishing gear, and each area has its own agreed unofficial protocols. Individuals can be fined up to $5000 for fishing outside of the notified season.

GATHERING REGIONAL PRODUCE AND LOCAL BEER

While Al worked the stand, Steve headed off to gather some other flavours of the region. In Westport, brewer Dean Lamplough pays tribute to coal miners with his selection of beers made at Miners' Brewery, including Denniston Draft Beer, Good Bastards Beer and their speciality light-tasting organic lager, Green Fern, which we decided would go down a treat back at the stand.

Over the hill from Mokihinui is the small settlement of Karamea, which has a mild micro-climate that's perfect for growing fruit and vegetables. Maggie MacBeth has a well-tended garden there and provided shallots, lemons and bay leaves for the butter sauce that we planned to serve with our whitebait. It was lovely for Steve to meet Maggie at last — her daughter Leila used to be a grill chef at Logan Brown for many years and had often talked about growing up in Karamea.

WELL DONE, BOY!

Sos told us that whitebaiting is all about putting in the time, 'If you don't put in the time, you miss out on the bait, simple as that.'

We knew we had to do our share of river time before T.O. would hand over the reins and give Al a go on the scoop net. River time consisted of watching Sos and T.O. patiently for what seemed like hours, presenting them with some local beer, listening to their stories and telling them a few yarns of our own. Eventually, T.O. stood aside to give us a turn — that's one hell of a kind gesture for a Coaster as keen on whitebaiting as he is.

With Al on the net it wasn't long before a few whitebait started to swim over the spotters and T.O. tutored him through the whole process. 'That's a good shoal down there, actually,' says T.O. 'Come up a bit, come up, bring the net up, keep going . . . slowly . . . move forward . . . keep going. That's a great little shoal . . . once the leaders run into the net they all follow . . . well done, boy!'

'It took a long time to get our whitebait, but when I did, it felt like I had struck gold, and it was time to prepare one of our favourite dishes,' said Al.

It's easy to fall in love with a spot like that stand on the Mokihinui River. Being able to cook the catch just two feet away from the river as it comes out of the water gives the word 'fresh' a completely new meaning, especially when the whitebait are still wriggling when they hit the pan.

We'd finally paid homage to this great New Zealand delicacy, enjoying it virtually leaping out of the river and into the pan. Meeting with some great characters, it was easy for us to understand why people do this day after day during the season.

A SHORT HISTORY OF THIS REGION

The tiny coastal township of Mokihinui, has a population of around 40 and is located midway between Westport and Karamea towards the northern end of the Coast.

Mokihi means 'a raft of dry flax stalks' and nui means 'big' so the name translates as 'big raft', suggesting the Mokihinui River was a difficult river to ford in earlier times.

Westport, population 4600, situated at the mouth of the Buller River, is the capital of the Buller region. Coal and gold were initially discovered in the region in 1859 by a surveyor, John Rochfort. Westport was established by goldminers in 1861. As the gold rush came to an end, coal became the main industry with mines in Denniston, Millerton and Stockton.

Maori first came to this region following greenstone or pounamu trails. A few settled here, including June Robinson's ancestors. We met June Robinson, of Ngati Apa, who told us of how her ancestors caught whitebait during the season and dried it so they had a year-round supply. They would dig trenches at strategic places in the river. The tide would push in and, usually around slack water, a kupenga or net made of closely woven flax was set across the trench so that the whitebait couldn't get out.

A gold town, called Kynnersley after the then resident commissioner, popped up briefly at the mouth of the river in 1867. It's now called Waimarie. The gold nuggets found there were called Mokihinui spuds because of their water-worn, flattened shape.

In 1879, an ingenious local, Robert Denniston, built the Denniston Incline to transport coal from the huge plateau above Granity to the base of the hill, 600 metres below. The incline was driven by pulleys and gravity — the loaded carts going down were used to haul the empty ones back up. The locals knew it as the 'eighth wonder of the world' and between 1879 and 1967 more than 13 million tonnes of coal was transported down the Incline.

The Mokihinui Bar is treacherous and the Mokihinui Coal Company's screw steamer, the SS *Lawrence*, foundered on the Mokihinui Bar on 28 April 1891. Today, the hull can still be seen at high-water mark, and the boiler is partly buried in sand 25 metres out to sea. The anchor sits right outside the Mokihinui Pub.

The coal industry is now in decline. Dairy, forestry and more recently, tourism are now important industries in the region and Westport also has New Zealand's largest cement works.

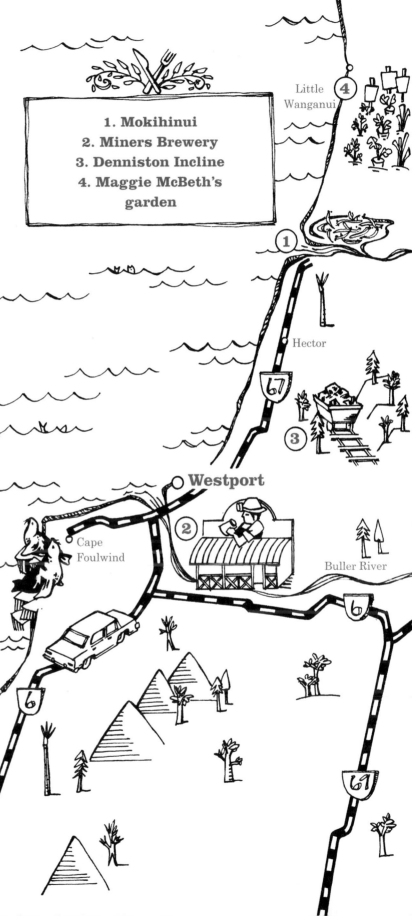

1. Mokihinui
2. Miners Brewery
3. Denniston Incline
4. Maggie McBeth's garden

Little Wanganui

Hector

Westport

Cape Foulwind

Buller River

SAUTÉED WHITEBAIT WITH FRESH ASPARAGUS AND BEURRE BLANC SAUCE By Al Brown

This dish is all about simplicity and not overpowering the delicate flavour of whitebait. It's always a celebration of that time of the year when the whitebait is running. If you don't have both, serve whitebait or asparagus, but putting the two ingredients together makes a terrific spring dish. This beurre blanc sauce with citrus through is a great combination for any seafood.

Serves 8 as an entrée.

STEP 1. BEURRE BLANC SAUCE

INGREDIENTS

50 ml white wine
50 ml white wine vinegar
1 shallot, roughly chopped
8 peppercorns
1 bay leaf

100 ml cream
250 g cold butter, cut into 1cm cubes
salt and pepper to season
squeeze of lemon juice (optional)

METHOD

Place the wine and vinegar in a saucepan and add the shallot, peppercorns and bay leaf. Place on medium heat and reduce the wine and vinegar by three-quarters. Add the cream and reduce by half. Cool slightly then return to very low heat. Whisk in the butter piece by piece until fully incorporated and the sauce has a silky smooth appearance. Strain the sauce through a fine sieve and discard the solids. Taste the beurre blanc sauce and season with salt and pepper and a squeeze of lemon juice, if required. The beurre blanc will keep in this form for a couple of hours if kept covered in a warm place. Once it's cold it can't be reheated as it will split.

STEP 2. PLATING AND SERVING

INGREDIENTS

40 asparagus spears
400 g whitebait, dried with paper towel
500 g flour
cooking oil

butter
salt and pepper to season
beurre blanc sauce
lemon wedges to garnish

METHOD

Place a large saucepan of salted water on high heat and when it is boiling, add the asparagus and cook for 4 to 5 minutes.

Meanwhile, take a skillet or sauté pan and bring up to high heat. In batches, place the dried whitebait in a dry sieve and cover with heaps of flour. Shaking the sieve, remove all the flour from the whitebait, leaving just a thin coating on each whitebait. Now add cooking oil and butter to the pan and immediately add the whitebait. Cook for about a minute on each side, until just golden. Remove and keep warm while you finish cooking the rest.

To serve, divide the cooked asparagus onto 8 warm plates and top with a sprinkling of sautéed whitebait. Spoon liberal amounts of the beurre blanc on each plate and garnish with a wedge of lemon.

STEVE'S WINE RECOMMENDATION

Nautilus Marlborough Pinot Gris

We matched this dish with this white wine variety related to Pinot Noir, which produces a spicy, aromatic, medium-bodied wine with a bit of fresh acidity. It's a good match for our relatively light dish of asparagus and whitebait sauté, as the wine's oily texture complements the buttery sauce, while its acidity cuts through the richness of the dish.

WILD RABBITS
IN CENTRAL OTAGO

THE ONLY GOOD RABBIT'S A DEAD ONE

It was a heck of a drive in the Holden as we made our way down through the stunning South Island landscapes to Central Otago.

Having heard stories over the years about rabbit plagues in Central Otago that were so bad that some farmers were driven off their land, we wanted to see what was going on these days and hunt down some furry pests for our wild rabbit and thyme stew.

It's big country down there — huge skies, vast surroundings and expansive properties. Wherever we looked we kept touching on how the first settlers must have endured incredible hardships. There are no green hills and the climate is harsh, ranging from sub-zero temperatures in winter, to extremely hot summers. The region probably has one of the lowest stock-units-per-acre ratios in the country and, even for one of the new breed of farmers there, viticulturists, it's considered to be one of the most fickle wine-growing regions of them all.

The early settlers and goldminers must have been as tough as old leather to cope with this environment. Those who did well did so because they were able to adapt to the land. Aside from a few large sheep stations there was very little significant European settlement in Central Otago until 1861, when the discovery of gold at Gabriels Gully led to a rapid influx of miners seeking their fortunes from those barren Central Otago hills. However, when the gold ran out many miners moved on.

As we drove into Central it became clear that many of the things we saw out the window were introduced by miners and farmers when the region was first settled, including thyme, rosehips and, of course, rabbits.

BUN'S PATCH

The guys needed four rabbits for their rabbit and thyme stew. Al reckoned that because he grew up on a farm he had the right credentials for the job. That suited Steve who wanted to get stuck into Central's stunning wines, unravel a bit of the region's history, and source some of the ingredients needed for their dish.

Al knew enough about the crafty rabbit to realise he needed some expert local knowledge, so he called in Bun (Ray) Scott, who's been chasing down rabbits for over 65 years.

Bun's patch is Bannockburn, just up the road from Cromwell, where he retired from full-time rabbiting about 18 years ago. Gold was discovered at Bannockburn in 1862 and the mining has left a lasting imprint on the landscape. It must be one of the most barren, dug-over and hole-ridden places Al and Steve visited, but it looked like an excellent place for finding rabbits.

Here they were in an area that's incredibly arid with burrows everywhere with a local legend whose name is Bun. 'I'd hate to think how many rabbits he's exterminated over the years,' said Al.

'Bun's foxies, Spot and Toy, were our best bet for flushing the rabbits out. Fox terriers are terrific little hunters. They're compact, have a good turn of pace, can get into tight little situations like burrows and they'll go and go all day,' said Al.

'And you still love doing this, after all these years, out with your dogs?'

'Yeah, yeah,' replied Bun. 'It's the one thing, you know — all my life until the day I go — I'll still have my dog and my gun and go rabbiting. Even though I've done all those years rabbiting, I've never lost interest in it. You know what though? The only good rabbit's a dead one!'

After hearing about the rabbit problems in Central Otago for so long, when it came time to catch one, there were none to be found — possibly because rabbits prefer the night. However, after Spot sniffed and rustled one out from a bramble bush, our first chance of securing dinner appeared.

'For some reason it was very quiet and it wasn't until Spotty flushed one out that Bun was able to take his shotgun to his shoulder. The next thing I heard was, "Bugger!" Our only chance at a good shot and Bun had forgotten to take the safety catch off. The rabbit scarpered.

'Normally Bun hunts by himself, but there he was with me, with that extra pressure to get a rabbit. It's a bit like showing someone how to cook something that you've done a million times and burning it — it's a slightly embarrassing situation. I was feeling for him big time,' said Al.

It was time to rethink the hunting strategy.

A CUPPA WITH BUN AND EILEEN

We headed back to Bun's in Cromwell for a cuppa. Bun and Eileen have been married for over 50 years and they know how to make a good cup of tea.

Eileen is so sprightly and onto it for her age, kindly welcoming us into her meticulously clean and organised kitchen. She's maintained that heart-warming tradition of always offering morning or afternoon tea and the opportunity for a good catch up.

The inviting aroma of her home cooking is the best welcome, even before greetings are exchanged. Taken for granted for so many years, this kind of hospitality has gained a new appreciation today. 'There's something simple and satisfying about sitting down with cup of tea, and some fresh baking,' says Al. Making preserves, bottling fruit and baking were once mainstays of our New Zealand cuisine, but we've been losing that tradition for a long time.

There's a terrific bond between Bun and Eileen — their lives have been one of partnership and dealing with the hardships that Central Otago has thrown at them over the years. Hanging out with them and listening to all their stories felt like capturing a piece of the country's history as they described how the region had taken shape.

When they first married, Bun and Eileen spent several years in a rabbiter's hut at the Roaring Meg on the Kawarau River, without electricity and many of the basics we all now take for granted. As Bun would be out hunting all day and half the night, Eileen would be on her own and, later, with small children. For her, there were lonely times.

Bun is someone who's lived in Central Otago all his life and loved it. His work has always revolved around rabbits. He's worked as a trapper, as well as for the rabbit boards, mainly implementing poisoning regimes. When he retired he went on to tackle the rabbit problems that occur in the vineyards.

Despite two hip operations and being in his late seventies, Bun's still as staunch as the land itself. He exhibits a real kindness and an old-fashioned politeness seldom seen these days.

Even though he's retired and not quite as agile as he used to be, Bun still goes hunting with his prized foxies. He's not about to put his feet up. Besides, with the type of spread Eileen regularly puts on, including her delicious crumbed rabbit, he's most unlikely to fade away.

EILEEN SCOTT'S CRUMBED RABBIT

Food to Eileen and Bun is all about sustenance. During their years working together in harsh climatic conditions, Eileen's great cooking has provided the much-needed fuel to keep them both going.

Bun and Eileen regularly eat rabbit. If there's a community 'do' on, it will be Eileen's plate of fried rabbit that gets cleaned up first. Like chicken, it tastes delicious, hot or cold, so it's ideal for a pot-luck spread.

Makes 6–8 pieces per rabbit.

INGREDIENTS
1 rabbit, skinned and gutted
salt
1 cup flour
3 eggs, beaten
1½ cups breadcrumbs
⅓ cup cooking oil

METHOD
To prepare the rabbit, remove the front and back legs. Keep the front legs whole but cut the back legs in half cutting through the joint. Take the remainder of the rabbit frame and chop through the backbone to get two nice pieces with the fillet attached. Discard the rest of the carcass.

Soak the rabbit pieces in water with a good pinch of salt added for at least 4 hours in the fridge.

Strain off the salted water and add fresh water, again with a good pinch of salt added. Bring the rabbit up to the boil and simmer for 20 minutes. Remove the rabbit pieces and while they are still warm dip them in flour, then egg and, finally, breadcrumbs.

In a skillet or frying pan heat up the oil and cook the crumbed rabbit pieces until golden on all sides.

Serve hot or cold.

GATHERING REGIONAL PRODUCE AND WINE

The dramatic Otago landscape with its harsh climate produces some of the most beautiful things — gold, stone fruit, Pinot Noir and thyme.

While Al was chasing rabbits, Steve went to collect the other ingredients to give their meal a distinctively Central flavour.

One of the earliest influences on Central Otago was the great goldrush of the 1860s that saw thousands of miners flocking to the barren Central Otago hills to seek their fortunes. But those that came had to find their gold on empty stomachs, there was very little food to be found anywhere.

Trout hadn't been introduced into the rivers, there were no pigs or goats in the hills and at that stage even rabbits were thin on the ground.

Brett Petrie at the Goldfields Mining Centre told us that most miners were poor and many lived on a staple of damper. Made out of flour and salt mixed with water, the dough is flattened out and cooked over a grate or hot plate. Steve was told that some of the miners were so hungry that they couldn't wait to cook the mixture and would eat the dough raw.

He also told Steve that with a lack of fresh fruit and vegetables, scurvy was a common problem among the miners, until their saviour, the briar rose, was introduced. Thriving well in the arid, harsh Central Otago soils, its rosehips — which look like little chillies — are an excellent source of vitamin C, and were boiled up into rosehip tea, providing the life-saving means of preventing scurvy.

Brett ran through how to make damper, which would make a good gravy soaker for our wild rabbit stew.

Central Otago is famous throughout New Zealand for its stone fruit. Its extreme weather — cold winters for setting flowers, followed by hot and dry summers for ripening fruit — are conducive to producing great peaches, apricots, cherries and many other varieties of stone fruit.

Many of the old fruit trees were planted by miners who may have taken gold, but in return, left something equally valuable — water. There's a network of dams and tail races around the region that were used to transport and store water for mining and to irrigate nearby gardens and fruit trees.

Pauline Murphy and Jane Shaw of Provisions in Old Cromwell Town make the most of local fruits, incorporating them into a range of jams, relishes, chutneys and fruit vinegars. Their signature product, Central Otago cherries in Pinot Noir syrup, tastes divine. The cherries still have a bit of bite to the texture and would make a wicked garnish for the rabbit stew.

Provisions also use local wild thyme in many of their recipes, including wild thyme mustard and thyme shortbread. You don't need to look closely around the Central Otago landscape to find masses of thyme growing wildly over large parts of this region.

Being a woody, fragrant, hardy bush, thyme is well suited to the environment, seeming like it has been there forever. Even the perfume of thyme suits the aridity of the area.

Probably introduced by miners during the goldrush, common thyme (*Thymus vulgaris*) was used for herbal and medicinal purposes and was once harvested, dried and sold by several local factories in Clyde and Roxburgh, then sent all over New Zealand. Cutting thyme was a source of pocket money for local kids, right up until the 1970s, after which dried thyme could be imported for significantly less than the price of the local product.

Local farmer Earl Atfield was one of those kids who cut thyme back then, but now his farm is overrun with it. 'Over a 70-year period, thyme has spread from the Clyde cemetery right out east,' he told Steve. 'Physically and economically I don't know how we can get rid of it. We've tried burning faces of it and it just grows back twice as thick the next year.'

Many farmers, like Earl, have lost thousands of acres of good pasture to

thyme. 'I could feel the farmers' frustrations because, ironically, even if they wanted to harvest thyme, there's just not the technology or cheap labour to process it,' said Steve, pointing to a clump. 'In Wellington that's about eight bunches of herbs at five bucks each — 40 bucks worth of thyme, thanks very much!'

'I'm a millionaire, mate,' Earl replied with a wry smile.

CHASING RABBITS

We still needed our four rabbits and, after being skunked with Bun, the pressure was on for Al. Luckily full-time rabbiter Billy Linwood agreed to take Al night-shooting — dusk is a good time for spotting rabbits as they tend to come out to feed into the night. Carrying on the tradition of both his father and grandfather, Billy loves rabbiting and he is one of four rabbiters who works the district full time.

'Being brought up on a Wairarapa farm, the idea that people could make a living out of rabbiting was my idea of a dream job,' said Al. 'Ending up cooking them for a living is about as close as I've got to that, and spending time with people who are living out my childhood dream is slightly ironic.'

Rabbits are prolific breeders. Despite decades of poisoning with 1080 and the covert introduction of rabbit calicivirus disease (RCD) in 1997, plagues of rabbits are ruining Central Otago's grassland and the need for full-time rabbiters to keep the population at bay continues, especially now there are signs that rabbits are bait-shy and becoming resistant to RCD.

'I don't think there's an ultimate rabbiting programme,' Billy told Al while they were out spotting rabbits from his ute. 'Where poisons are still working effectively that's fine. Where RCD's working effectively that's fine as well, but you've still got to have all those other follow-up things, like some dogging and night-shooting, to keep the numbers as low as possible. It's got to be a whole mix of everything. But you'll never get the last rabbit.'

Billy does most of his shooting at night. He starts at around nine o'clock and tours various properties, knocking over rabbits by himself. Rabbiters obviously enjoy their own company, love the land and their dogs, and are completely driven to get rid of them.

'We spent a few hours that night driving over rugged country in Billy's four-wheel-drive, spotting rabbits with a hand-held torch and taking turns at getting behind the barrel of Billy's 22-calibre rifle. Billy's a crack shot living up to his reputation and soon we were heading back with our bag of rabbits.' To watch someone who is so steady and accurate at such long range is a real treat, according to Al.

CENTRAL OTAGO PINOT NOIR

No story of this region is complete without a mention of Pinot Noir. A notoriously fickle and difficult grape to cultivate, some wine experts say that the best Pinot Noir in the country should be grown in the Otago region, but not necessarily every year.

A Frenchman, Jean Desire Feraud, is thought to have been the first person to plant vines in Central Otago in the late 1880s. Having struck it lucky as a goldminer in an area now known as Frenchman's Point, he was smart enough to realise that the real money lay with the miners, not the mining. A great entrepreneur, he purchased 110 acres (44.5 hectares), gained water rights and planted fruit trees and grapevines. By 1870, he was producing wines at the stone winery he established called Monte Christo. It must have been a good drop because it won medals when he exhibited it in Sydney. Unfortunately for Feraud, the beer-drinking miners didn't appreciate his wines and Feraud sold the property in 1882 and moved to Dunedin.

In 1895, Yugoslav-born, French- and Italian-trained viticulturist Romeo Bragato, who was government viticulturist from 1902–09, explored the region. He is famously reported to have said, 'There is no better country on the face of this earth for the production of Burgundy grapes than Central Otago.' He also commented on how wonderfully laden all the fruit trees were in the region. However, expert as he was, he failed to change the thinking of

pauline, jane
and steve

bun and eileen

billy and al

steve and duncan
at mt edward

the musterers' hut

dinner with otago
rabbiters

Duncan: Central Otago has hot days and cold nights, not moderated by the seas, which crucially help the grapes intensify their fruit flavours and colour. These are also helped by clear skies and long days, which produce a light-intensity second to none. The soil types, which are a combination of clay and schist, help provide structure, texture and a desirable mineral character to the wines. The region's cold, dry air makes it hard for bugs and bacteria to survive.

New Zealanders, who were not convinced that there was a viable economic future in wine production.

Even though the Central Otago region was recognised as an area of great potential for growing Burgundy-style grapes as far back as the late 1800s, it wasn't until almost a century later, in 1981, that the first serious plantings were made, creating a new rush in Central Otago.

The first commercial release of pinot noir in Central Otago was by Alan Brady at Gibbston Valley Winery in 1987. Today, it's estimated that more than 700 hectares of grapes — and growing — are planted in this region and more than 70 per cent of the plantings are pinot noir. It's the southern-most wine-making region in the world and has the highest vineyards in New Zealand, with plantings between 200 and 400 metres above sea level. In the overall picture of wine production, Central Otago produces only a tiny percentage of New Zealand's wine production, yet wines from the region have an almost cult-like status, both locally and internationally.

Steve paid a visit to his good friend Duncan Forsyth at Mt Edward Vineyard who says that Central Otago has the right combination of climate and soil.

The people behind the wines are just as important, too, and we were looking forward to tasting Duncan's outstanding Mt Edward Pinot Noir with our rabbit stew.

COOKING IN AN OLD MUSTERERS' HUT

With our rabbits in hand, we headed to an old musterers' hut at Earnscleugh Station, to cook the rabbit for Bun, Billy and a couple of other local rabbiters. The Holden wasn't quite up to the job, so we got there by four-wheel-drive and an uphill hike.

The old hut is used as a resting point and sleepout for the sheep musterers and rabbiters. It's a stone building with two simple rooms, a fire, and inscriptions carved into the wood and stone. Over the years, people who've camped out there have carved their names and the date of their stay into the exposed framework. Running water consisted of a stream nearby. We were going to be cooking exactly how they would have done years ago with a Dutch oven (a heavy cast-iron pot with a lid) sitting over the grate of the fire. It was perfect for cooking our stew long and slow.

What a dining room — a rustic stone hut with a dirt floor, low ceiling and candles providing our only light. Huddled around the table with rugged rabbiters for company, delicious heart-warming rabbit stew and divine pinot noir, makes for an unforgettable experience. Knowing we'd done our bit for the rabbit eradication programme made it all the more satisfying.

WILD RABBITS

Central Otago is the most rabbit-prone region in the country.

Wild rabbits are thought to have been first introduced from Australia in around 1838, to provide British settlers with game for hunting.

They eat grasses, young flower buds, clover, seeds, young grapevines, but not thyme. They do need to drink water, but are able to source most of what they need through the food they consume, allowing them to thrive even in Central Otago's dry conditions.

Rabbits tend to be largely nocturnal, resting under cover during the day in 'stops' or warrens, which are up to one-metre long, with just one opening. The stops are built by the does. Tunnels are less common. The rabbits block the holes to keep out predators.

With a short gestation period of only 30 days, females can reproduce many times a year.

The peak birthing seasons follow green grass in late spring and autumn, with breeding tailing off after Christmas as grasslands dry off in the summer heat.

When first introduced, rabbit numbers appeared to grow slowly, as they struggled to survive on Central Otago's long grasses. By the 1870s short-grazed pasture was developed, providing better food for sheep and rabbits, promoting a population explosion to occur. A flourishing export trade in rabbit skin developed, with canned and frozen rabbit meat also later traded.

Although the rabbit trade was thriving, the damage to land was catastrophic. Extensive erosion was a common occurrence, blamed on rabbits stripping the hills of vegetative growth. Sheep were competing for the same food source, making farming less economic.

District rabbit boards were set up in 1938 to kill rabbits all year around and not just for the fur and meat trade. In 1947, the government passed legislation establishing a Rabbit Destruction Council to deal with the rabbit plague. The council deliberately devalued rabbit skins and meat dramatically, making it illegal for the rabbit trade to continue. This was done to prevent people from breeding more rabbits to supply the trade.

In the 1980s the district rabbit boards were disestablished with the responsibility for rabbit control being put back on the farmers. Farmers looked for cheap ways to control numbers but rabbit populations grew exponentially again, and while there was a call for the disease myxomatosis to be introduced. Many people objected to the idea due to the fact that rabbits could take up to two weeks to die.

In the 1990s, South Island farmers were calling for the introduction of RCD, or rabbit calicivirus disease, but the government denied approval for it due to uncertainty about its long-term effectiveness and possible environmental effects. A group of farmers smuggled the virus in and released it in 1997. This resulted in a huge drop in rabbit numbers.

A SHORT HISTORY OF THIS REGION

New Zealand's most inland region it's an area of approximately 10,000 square kilometres with a total population of less than 17,000 permanent residents.

It is also the hottest, coldest and driest region in the country. A fragmented schist plateau in a semi-desert environment, Central Otago is scattered with historic features that have been preserved by the dry climate. It's a peaceful, powerful place that offers physical challenges and seasonal contrasts.

Because of the extreme climatic conditions, Maori travelled great distances to hunt and gather food. In summer and autumn, Central Otago was a hunting ground for eel, waterfowl and other birds, including the now extinct moa. It was also on the route to the West Coast for gathering pounamu or greenstone.

European settlements started to form in the 1850s when land was able to be leased. However, most of the early development of Central Otago was as a result of the goldrushes, including the establishment of Cromwell, Clyde, Alexandra and Roxburgh. Goldminers arrived seeking their fortunes after Gabriel Read discovered gold in 1861.

Many miners came from the goldfields of North America and Australia. However, by the late nineteenth century, 40 per cent of all miners in Central Otago were Chinese.

Harnessing water is very important for the region, with hydro-electric dams bringing environmental change and employment to the region, most recently the Clyde dam built between 1977 and 1992.

The wine industry began to take off in the 1980s and Central Otago Pinot Noir is highly sought after in select global markets.

Today, while horticulture and agriculture continue to form the basis of the local economy, viticulture and tourism are making a growing and significant contribution.

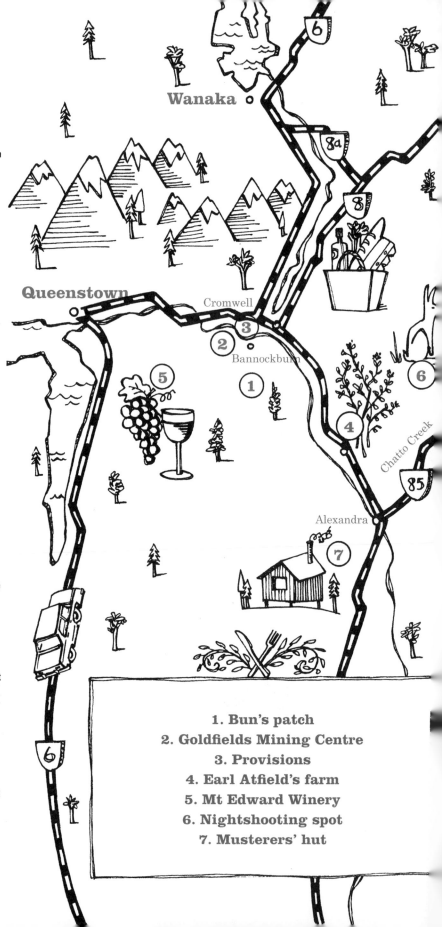

1. Bun's patch
2. Goldfields Mining Centre
3. Provisions
4. Earl Atfield's farm
5. Mt Edward Winery
6. Nightshooting spot
7. Musterers' hut

SEARED WILD RABBIT FILLETS WITH HONEY MUSTARD VINAIGRETTE By Al Brown

The two fillets or backstraps are the only parts of a rabbit that can be cooked medium-rare. Cooked quickly on high heat, the fillets are very tender.

Serves 8 as an entrée.

INGREDIENTS
$^1/_3$ cup honey
1 tablespoon Dijon mustard
1 tablespoon wholegrain mustard
4 tablespoons cider vinegar
½ cup canola oil, extra to cook rabbit
salt and pepper to season
4 wild rabbit fillets

METHOD
Pour the honey, mustards and cider vinegar into a bowl and whisk until incorporated. While whisking, slowly drizzle in the canola oil until emulsified and thick. Season with salt and pepper.

Place a frying pan or skillet on a high heat. Season rabbit fillets with salt and pepper. Add a little cooking oil to the pan.

Cook the rabbit fillets until golden, approximately 2 to 4 minutes on each side. Remove and rest for a couple of minutes.

Slice and arrange on a platter. Drizzle over vinaigrette. Serve with damper or crusty bread and thyme mustard or an array of chutneys.

WILD RABBIT & THYME STEW WITH KUMARA FONDANT By Al Brown

Rabbiters need a big feed on their plates and it needs to be hearty fare. With any wild game, besides the primary fillet cuts that you cook quickly, you'll get the most out of it if you cook it slowly. As with a lot of game, our rabbits were incredibly lean so long, slow cooking to break down the muscles until tender and concentrate the flavours was what was needed.

This rabbit stew with smoked bacon and fresh vegetables has Central Otago written all over it. It's wonderful winter fare and a regional dish in every sense — hunting the rabbits, picking the wild thyme and serving the stew with local sweet potatoes, and some stone fruit that had been poached in Pinot Noir made for a perfect match of regional wine and food.

Serves 8 as a main.

STEP 1. WILD RABBIT AND THYME STEW

INGREDIENTS

2 wild rabbits skinned and gutted
$1/_3$ cup cooking oil
250 g smoked bacon, roughly chopped
500 g onion, peeled and roughly chopped
150 g celery, roughly chopped
250 g carrot, peeled and roughly chopped
10 garlic cloves, peeled and roughly chopped

¼ cup freshly picked wild thyme, minced
2 bay leaves
2 cups red wine (preferably a good-quality pinot noir)
3 cups chicken stock
1 cup beef demi-glaze
50 g butter
50 g flour

METHOD

Remove the front and back legs from each rabbit, followed by the two fillets that run along the back of the rabbit frames. These fillets can be used to garnish the stew or used in another recipe, as we did. The front legs have a bit more bone but they have plenty of flavour.

Heat a Dutch oven or heavy pan with lid to high heat and add the oil and then the rabbit legs. Sear all over until nice and golden. Remove rabbit from the pan and set aside. While the pan is still hot, add the chopped bacon and cook until caramelised. Add the onion, celery, carrot, garlic, thyme and bay leaves. Sauté the vegetables with the bacon until they also colour.

Return the rabbit legs to the pan and pour over the red wine, chicken stock and demi-glaze.

Cover the pan and cook in a moderate to low oven (150–200°C) for about 2 hours.

Check the rabbit to see if it is cooked. It should come away from the bone with ease and be very tender. If not, check at 20 minute intervals until cooked.

Carefully strain off the cooking liquid and leave the cooked rabbit and vegetables in the pan. Put the butter in another saucepan over medium heat. Once melted, add the flour and whisk until incorporated. Pour in the cooking liquid while whisking and whisk until sauce has thickened with no lumps. Pour the sauce back over the cooked rabbit and keep warm until required.

STEP 2. KUMARA FONDANT

INGREDIENTS
1 kg golden kumara
3 cups chicken stock
100 g butter, roughly chopped

METHOD
Peel the kumara and cut into 1-cm thick discs. Place the discs in a single layer into skillets or sauté pans. Pour over the chicken stock until it just covers the kumara. Arrange the butter evenly over the kumara and stock. Place the pans on medium heat. The kumara will start to absorb the stock and butter. Once all the stock has been absorbed, all that is left will be clarified butter. Turn the kumara over and cook for another 5 minutes until golden around the edges. Remove the pans from the heat and let the kumara sit for about 10 minutes. This creates a nice crust that comes away with the kumara when you remove it from the pan. Remove kumara fondant from the pan and store in an airtight container in the fridge until required.

STEP 3. PLATING AND SERVING

INGREDIENTS
Rabbit stew
Kumara fondant
Provisions' cherries in Pinot Noir syrup (optional garnish)

METHOD
Heat the rabbit stew in the oven or on the stove top over low heat and heat the kumara fondant until warmed through. On hot plates place a couple of pieces of kumara. Spoon plenty of gravy over portions of rabbit. Garnish with a few cherries in Pinot Noir syrup, if using, and serve immediately. Some crusty fresh bread and a green salad would round out this dish perfectly!

AL'S TIPS ON HOW TO BREAK DOWN A RABBIT

- Lay the rabbit carcass flat on a chopping board. Remove back legs.

- Remove the front legs.

- Two front legs, two back legs and whole rabbit saddle.

- Run your knife along each side of the backbone to remove the two rabbit fillets.

- Rabbit fillets suit fast, quick cooking, rabbit legs suit long, slow cooking and for the rabbit carcass, roast until golden brown and use for stock or perhaps soup.

   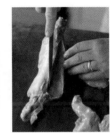 

STEVE'S WINE RECOMMENDATION

Mount Edward Pinot Noir

This Otago Pinot Noir lends itself to the wild rabbits that flourish in the scrubby thyme-covered hills of Central Otago. It's got both savoury and sweet characteristics, often with hints of thyme and cherries, which naturally complement game meats. Pinot Noir tends to be more medium bodied with fine tannins that don't overpower a relatively delicate meat like rabbit.

PAUA ON THE
WAIRARAPA COAST

PAUA BUTTIES ON THE BEACH

We headed over the hill from Wellington to Castlepoint on the Wairarapa Coast to indulge in one of our all-time favourites — paua butties on the beach, washed down with some of the region's finest wine.

Paua, New Zealand's native species of abalone, grow around the rocky coasts of many parts of the country. For us, they have the same iconic status as crayfish, whitebait and Bluff oysters.

When we opened Logan Brown Restaurant over a decade ago, very few other restaurants were serving paua, probably because of its astronomical price. We created our entrée, paua ravioli with lime beurre blanc, as an economical way of including this high-priced delicacy on the menu. It gave us a real point of difference and is now one of our signature dishes.

The obvious place to go for our paua was Castlepoint on the rugged Wairarapa coastline, which is well known for its seafood and is only a few hours drive from Wellington.

Al was lucky enough to have grown up on a Wairarapa farm, but for Steve, travelling from Wellington, it was a daunting trip as a youngster. For years, the windy road over the 900-metre-high Rimutaka Ranges, guarded the Wairarapa from visiting Wellingtonians. Getting over the hills when Steve was a boy meant carefully negotiating a long, narrow, twisting road, with frightening drops down one side, often buffeted by gale-force winds and even the occasional snow flurry. Inevitably, there were stops to relieve carsickness and break up back-seat rumbles, but reaching the summit provided relief for all as the valley below opened up to reveal the welcoming, big, blue skies of the Wairarapa. Now, with modern cars and better roads, the trip is a cinch and many people commute daily between the provinces.

It was about an hour's drive past Featherston in the Holden through small towns and increasingly isolated farmland out to the coast at Castlepoint Beach, where the young Al spent his summer holidays.

By the time we arrived we were keen to get out, explore the area and taste some of the delicious seafood on offer. Al claimed the right to go for the paua, so it was Steve who went off to explore the region and rustle up the other ingredients for our paua-buttie cook-up on the beach.

AL'S CAMPING HOLIDAYS AT CASTLEPOINT

Going back to this region always strikes a chord with Al. Some of his earliest memories of gathering paua were during family holidays at Castlepoint camping ground, where he stayed in an old wooden caravan nicknamed 'the pie cart'.

Each day revolved around low tide. Families would pile into their station wagons and head off along the gravel road over the hill, to the rugged and rocky Mataikona Coast. The mums would throw down rugs and set up a picnic, while dads donned wetsuits to snorkel for crayfish. The kids went exploring the rock pools, looking for large paua — in those days they could be found in knee-deep water — to prise off the rocks with screwdrivers. It was like the hide 'n' seek of hunting and gathering. 'I still remember the buzz I got at the age of four when I found a huge paua and knew I was contributing to the family meal.'

In those days you could just about guarantee that the dads would come back with a few crays too. It was thirsty work and they'd pull up a crate of beer anchored in the water to cool. Content, they'd sit back and watch the tide come in. The kids were rewarded for their work too, with a sip of the froth off the top of the beer.

After returning to the camping ground, the paua was shucked and put through a mincer, which was clamped to a Formica table next to the caravan. The paua would then be made into fritters. The old boiler would be cranked up for the crays, and any fish that had been caught during the day would be gutted and filleted ready for the nightly feed of kaimoana.

'This was my first experience of the excitement that the anticipation of hunting and gathering generates and I was hooked.'

CASTLEPOINT BEACH

Castle Point was named by Captain Cook as he sailed by in 1770 because he thought the large prominent rock resembled a castle. Today, Castlepoint Beach is a popular holiday destination, well known for its lighthouse, good reef fishing, surfing and horse races on the beach.

The camping ground Al stayed at as a kid is still there and there's a boat club and an increasing number of baches. The pub is a few kilometres up the road and there's a general store that provides basic supplies to locals and tourists alike.

The lighthouse is a prominent feature and further north of it there's a long, expansive beach. To the south, a horseshoe-shaped reef creates a safe lagoon for swimming and, on the ocean side, there's great fishing to be had.

CATCHING A KAHAWAI

Steve thought some smoked kahawai would be a nice treat for the paua divers when they returned, so before heading off to collect the other ingredients, he bought some bait from the store and headed to the reef.

The reef at Castle Point is famous for its fishing, but also infamous for the deaths and injuries that occur when people are swept off the rocks by rogue waves. Steve wandered up past the warning signs and planted himself next to a guy who had a freshly caught kahawai lying on the rock next to him. Like most of the locals, he was a friendly guy and it wasn't long before he and Steve had struck up a conversation.

His name was Alan Schofield and he'd been coming to the reef to fish for as long as he could remember. 'Fisherman are always pleased to have a yarn about their luck — the one that got away, the weather conditions and even their bait. It's all part of the day's experience,' says Steve.

Alan's father used to catch huge groper off this reef as big as the then three-year-old Alan. That size of catch has almost disappeared, but there are still plenty of fish to be had and kahawai are easily caught on the hook.

They're a great game fish and always put up a fight. Steve bled the kahawai immediately to prevent blood from colouring and spoiling the flesh.

MATAI AND KURA

Leaving Steve, Al headed up the coast to the mouth of the Mataikona River where he crossed a rickety swing-bridge to meet Matai Broughton. Matai is based at the southern end of Owahanga Station where he's been since the 1970s. With a broad, open smile, Matai removed his hat before shaking hands with Al — an old-fashioned courtesy that's often overlooked these days.

North from Mataikona River mouth Owahanga Station follows more than ten kilometres of rugged coastline. When much of the land in the Castlepoint area was divided and sold to European farmers back in 1853, local Maori kept a piece at Owahanga that has never been sold. Matai's great-grandfather was one of the chiefs who signed the original deed and so it is fitting that Matai is now kaitiaki, or guardian, of this coastline.

The remoteness of this piece of the coast makes for some great paua collecting and Matai had a special spot in mind a few k's up the coast. But, with low tide a couple of hours away, he suggested he take Al home to meet his wife Kura and try some of her paua dishes.

Kura has been cooking paua for much of her life and her creamed paua is legendary. Al was keen to try it, but it came at a price — he had to be her kitchen hand.

Al helped Kura combine the ingredients for her amazingly rich and tasty creamed paua, which can be served as a dip or even a sauce for fish or pasta. Kura served the creamed paua with paua chips and deep-fried dumplings called floaters.

KURA'S CREAMED PAUA DIP, FLOATERS AND PAUA CHIPS

STEP 1. CREAMED PAUA

INGREDIENTS
2 tablespoons butter
2 cloves garlic, minced
1 medium-sized onion, finely chopped
4 minced paua
300 ml cream
flour or cornflour to thicken
salt and pepper to taste
lemon juice to taste

METHOD
Heat saucepan, add the butter, garlic and onion and cook until golden brown. Add paua and toss for 1 minute, then add cream and thicken with flour or cornflour. Season with salt, pepper and lemon juice.

STEP 2. FLOATERS

INGREDIENTS
2 cups self-raising flour
2 cups water (more or less)
oil for deep frying

METHOD
Mix flour and water to make a nice dough. Roll small bits of dough into balls and drop into very hot oil. Fry until a nice golden brown. Drain on greaseproof paper before serving with the creamed paua.

STEP 3. PAUA CHIPS

INGREDIENTS
4 paua sliced into thin strips
flour to coat paua
2 tablespoons butter

METHOD
Pat the paua strips dry with a paper towel and put into a plastic bag with a little flour. Shake until every strip is lightly covered with flour. Heat butter to very hot in a frying pan and cook paua until golden brown.

SNORKELLING FOR PAUA WITH MATAI

Matai and Kura were so welcoming it would have been easy to relax at their home all day, but Al had paua to gather and, with low tide approaching, it was time to head on out. Matai's spot was a quad-bike ride away over a rough, four-wheel-drive farm track. He and Al wound their way up a huge hill and at the top were rewarded with stunning views in every direction.

Looking north towards the paua grounds, Matai and Al could see the rugged coastline disappearing into a distant sea fog. With the smell of salt and the anticipation of a few fresh paua, Matai wasted no time on the trip down the hill and once he'd hit the sand, he throttled up the empty beach. 'It doesn't come much better than that,' reckoned Al.

Paua used to be common right around New Zealand, but pressure from overfishing and poaching has reduced the availability and protected spots like this are few and far between.

There was a slight swell kicking up a bit of sand. 'She's a bit dirty, mate, she's a bit dirty,' said Matai, surveying the water. Often it's the weather and murky conditions that protect the resource, but Matai managed to find a bit of water sheltered by a reef.

Jumping into wetsuits and snorkelling gear, Matai and Al headed into the water. It was freezing, but the colder the water, the larger the paua — or so they say — so it was something they were happy to put up with.

Matai and Al spent the good part of an hour foraging in the cold Wairarapa waters. The visibility was marginal at best, but there were plenty of large paua, which they found by running a hand under and along the prominent ledges. It was a real contrast to many parts of New Zealand where you have to work hard to find enough legal-sized paua for a feed these days.

Matai and Al dropped the paua into a bag, before returning to the quad bike, feeling cold but exhilarated and looking forward to a damn good fire and some paua butties.

Al: There was something special about the trip over the hill with Matai and quite often on these trips it's like that — the journey becomes the real highlight. What you get at the end of the day is a bonus.

GATHERING LOCAL INGREDIENTS AND WINE

Fresh coriander is one of the main flavours of the paua butties which Steve needed to find. He also wanted to muster some rocket and a few lemons. Thanks to Alan Schofield's help on the reef at Castle Point, Steve already had freshly caught kahawai and Alan pointed him in the direction of his wife, Margie. She has a great garden — a necessity when you live so far from town. Good-old sliced white bread was next on Steve's list.

When Al and Steve were growing up, buttered, sliced white bread was a common addition to the table and it's a great way to make a meal go further.

PAUA

Paua are slow growing and take about 12 years to reach legal size. Large paua may be as much as 30 years old.

The row of holes in the shell is for breathing and breeding. Starfish can suffocate paua by closing the shellfish's breathing holes with their tentacles. The paua then have to let go of the rock.

During spawning, the females release millions of eggs and the males release sperm. They mix together in stormy autumn waters and once the eggs have been fertilised they hatch into microscopic larvae. About a week later they develop a shell and eventually attach themselves to a rock where they become an important part of the food chain, providing food for an array of sea life.

The most common paua in New Zealand is the black-footed paua, which must be 12.5 cm long before it can be harvested.

The catch limit for gathering paua is 10 per person per day.

Paua are haemophiliacs and if they are accidentally nicked they can bleed to death. Therefore, it is best to measure them while they are still attached to rocks to avoid damaging under-sized fish.

It's also a great foil for savoury or sweet eating: with a sausage and sauce, it's dinner; with a smear of jam, it's breakfast or dessert.

At Breadcraft in Masterton, Steve met up with Craig Shanahan who showed him how they make bread today. Breadcraft is highly mechanised, with a capacity to make 3500 loaves an hour. The company supplies the local population and many other parts of New Zealand. It proudly traces its ownership back well over a century, to when Samuel Gapper established a flourmill in the region in the 1870s. Since then it has changed hands many times to become a thoroughly modern commercial bakery business. Next on the list was the wine.

There's nothing like a glass of chilled wine to go with paua butties and the Wairarapa, including Martinborough, is developing a great reputation internationally for its fine wines.

Grapes were first planted just outside of Masterton in 1883, but in 1908 the district voted for prohibition and the vines were all pulled out — there was no compensation for the growers and, probably, no sympathy, either.

It wasn't until the 1970s that a new generation of winemakers saw the potential of the region and began replanting. Now there are more than 50 vineyards in the Wairarapa, many of them still small, family-owned blocks.

One of these belongs to Paddy Borthwick, a long-time friend of Al and Steve. For more than a century the Borthwick family championed much of New Zealand's international meat exporting business. Now, a great-grandson of the original pioneering Borthwick, Paddy has established Borthwick Vineyard, which grows grapes on a stony river terrace at Gladstone.

Steve dropped in to see Paddy's cellar and, hearing about the paua butties, Paddy suggested a Riesling.

So with the wine, white bread, rocket, coriander, lemon and the kahawai all in hand, Steve headed back to Castlepoint to meet up with Al, Matai and Kura.

SMOKING KAHAWAI

There was just one job left for Steve and that was to smoke the kahawai. First, he gutted and scaled the fish then removed the centre bone. He smeared the flesh with salt and brown sugar. Using a portable smoker, he smoked the kahawai over manuka wood chips for about 20 minutes, until it was cooked and starting to flake.

Matai, Kura and Al pulled up at the beach on the quad bike, Steve produced the moist, smoked kahawai for everyone to enjoy. It went down a real treat.

COOK-UP ON THE BEACH

A successful beach cook-up depends a lot on choosing the right location — somewhere out of the wind with good comfortable seating. We found a great

preparing the kahawai
for the smoker

matai kura and al with some
of kura's famous paua dip

matai and al

steve and alan castlepoint reef

shucking the paua

sautéed paua

Al: The paua we're eating is only hours old. To catch it and cook it on a fire like this — nothing could be finer.

little spot in a hollow, with a nice big log to sit on. It was near a freshwater stream and there was plenty of driftwood to make a great fire.

What a beautiful place to dine. The smell of the sea, the smoky driftwood fire, the sounds of the gulls, the breeze and the sea, the colours of the beach and sky at twilight — it's these things that make eating outside such an enjoyable thing to do. Sharing the experience with Kura and Matai and their refreshingly old-fashioned courtesy, warmth of spirit and great sense of humour, we knew we were in wonderful company.

A SHORT HISTORY OF THIS REGION

Wairarapa means 'glistening waters' and is said to have been named by the Maori explorer Haunui.

During the Land Wars many Wairarapa Maori left to live in Taranaki, returning a decade later in 1841 to rebuild their villages.

Rangiwhakaoma was first discovered by the great Maori explorer Kupe who in stories is said to have been chasing a giant octopus all the way from Hawaiki when he found this sheltered bay. Later, Captain Cook named the place Castle Point.

The first European settler at Castlepoint was Thomas Guthrie, who arrived in 1841.

The first sheep in New Zealand were driven from Wellington around the southern coast in 1844, establishing New Zealand's first sheep station. Later, bales of wool were rowed out to ships for transportation back to Wellington.

In 1853–54 1.5 million acres (607,000 hectares), originally held by Wairarapa Maori, was purchased by the Crown. This included a 275,000-acre (111,000 hectares) block at Castlepoint.

The first road access to Wellington was opened in 1859.

In 1908 this area was one of the first in New Zealand to vote for prohibition.

The Castlepoint lighthouse was opened in 1913 and was one of the last manned lighthouses in New Zealand until it was automated in 1981.

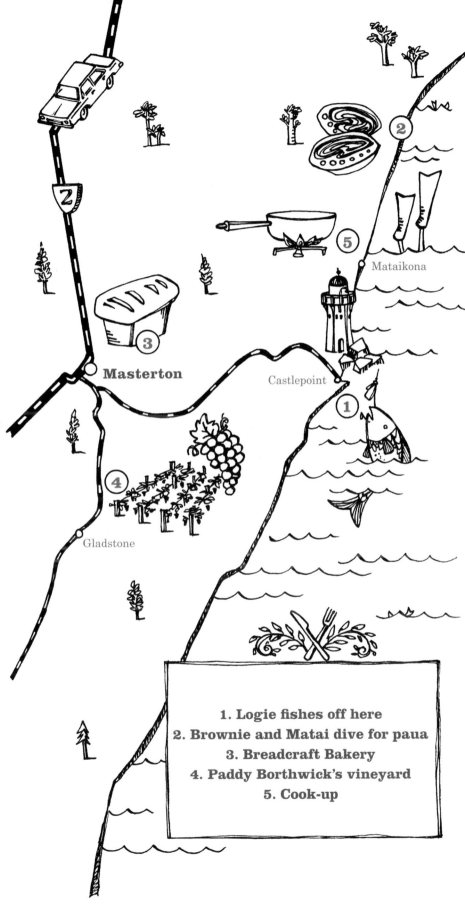

Mataikona

Castlepoint

Masterton

Gladstone

1. Logie fishes off here
2. Brownie and Matai dive for paua
3. Breadcraft Bakery
4. Paddy Borthwick's vineyard
5. Cook-up

PAUA BUTTIES By Al Brown

These paua butties are a modern interpretation of the paua fritters we used to have as kids, which generally comprised minced paua, some onion, egg and flour. In the camping ground way back when, there wouldn't have been a chilli, fresh coriander or rocket in sight!

Paua lends itself nicely to a very quick sauté, although it will always have a little bite and texture, but the rest of these ingredients complement it perfectly.

To prepare an open fire for cooking, let the fire burn down so that you get a nice, even heat from the embers.

Makes 8.

STEP 1. PAUA

INGREDIENTS
4 paua, sliced into thin strips
1 tablespoon minced garlic

METHOD
Slice the paua into thin slices. Add the garlic and mix together.

STEP 2. COOKING AND SERVING

INGREDIENTS
1 loaf of white bread
butter
prepared paua
canola oil or olive oil (for cooking)
1 small red onion, thinly sliced
1–2 red chillies, finely diced
½ cup fresh coriander, roughly chopped
salt and pepper, to season
1 lemon, halved
rocket

METHOD
Butter 16 slices for 8 sandwiches.

It is best to cook the paua in two batches. Heat a skillet, add a little oil, then the onion and cook until the onions have caramelised. Add the paua

and garlic mixture and sauté briefly (for no longer than a couple of minutes) before adding the chilli, coriander, a squeeze of lemon juice and a couple of tablespoons of butter. Cook for another 30 seconds. Season to taste and pile onto the buttered bread. Top with another slice of bread to complete the butties. Consume with abandon.

HOW TO SHUCK A PAUA

- There's a bit of a knack to shucking paua.

- First, run your thumb down the inside of the shell until you feel the paua muscle separate from the bottom of the shell.

- Next, run your thumb back onto the hua or guts and pull backwards. The hua should remain attached to the shell while the rest of the paua is easily pulled away.

- Remove the two white teeth at the end of the paua.

- Wash the paua in salt water and it is ready to go.

STEVE'S WINE RECOMMENDATION

Borthwick Vineyards Riesling from Gladstone
We matched the sautéed paua butties with Paddy Borthwick's Wairarapa Riesling. It's a medium-bodied off-dry style that won't overpower the butties. There's enough residual sugar to offset the heat of the chilli. The citrusy acidity will cleanse the palate between mouthfuls.

PHEASANTS IN ROTORUA

SWAN AROUND IN YOUR TWEEDS OR CHUCK ON YOUR SWANNI

In search of dinner fit for a king, we headed to Rotorua to experience the pheasant-shooting season and to track down some winter treats to make a decadent dish of pheasant. We planned to stuff a breast with fresh truffle and serve it with confit leg of pheasant and Jerusalem artichoke purée.

Rotorua, a popular geothermal area, is where hordes of tourists go to take in Maori culture and to inhale the sulphur fumes. But we were here for the pheasants.

There are two ways to hunt pheasant in New Zealand. You can put on your swanni and head for the wild, or pull on your tweeds and head for the preserve. Either way, these introduced swamp-birds are crafty, flighty and fast, which makes it a challenge to shoot them every time.

We were excited at the thought of hunting pheasants — not only are they beautiful birds, they're also great eating. Not surprisingly, we both favoured the idea of shooting pheasants on the preserve, where birds roam in the thousands and you're never far from a sherry and a great selection of savouries. Slogging it out in the wild didn't seem to have the same appeal.

We decided to sort it out by having a clay pigeon shoot-off. 'There was obviously something wrong with my gun because I hardly shot a thing, while Al was blasting them out of the air,' said Steve.

With the decision made, Al dropped Steve off to go hunting in the wild with local legend and pheasant-hunter Bill Teare, before heading off to source some ingredients for their dish.

PHEASANT HUNTING IN THE WILD

When Steve met up with Bill he was cleaning his shotgun in the shed down the back of his well-kept section. Sheds speak volumes about their owners and Steve had an immediate impression of Bill.

The walls were adorned with a huge range of tools, ribbons and hunting trophies, all meticulously arranged and laid out. Mounted on the wall were a boar's head and a stuffed pheasant and there was a locked fridge housing a selection of beautifully maintained hunting guns. Everything had its place.

It was no surprise to learn that Bill Teare had been hunting most of his life and was in no hurry to give up. Happily retired, Bill can pick and choose his hunting days and his wife, Grace, always sends him off with a basket of baking and a hot thermos to keep him going.

Steve and Bill headed off to one of Bill's favourite hunting grounds in Rotoehu Forest, an hour-and-a-half's drive through developed farmland and exotic forestry east of Rotorua.

In England, pheasant shooting has always been the exclusive preserve of the upper classes, but when pheasants were introduced into New Zealand, the early settlers were determined to make hunting them the right of every New Zealander. After initially thriving, pheasant numbers rapidly declined and for more than a hundred years, Acclimatisation Societies worked hard to build-up numbers in the wild, without a lot of success. The decline in numbers was probably due to introduced predators, and the loss of habitat, as a result of pastoral development.

Pheasants tend to stay close to the ground and are experts at hiding, which is why you need to take along a good game dog. Bill has an English pointer called Bud,whose job is to sniff out a pheasant, point it out and then flush it into the air so that Bill can get a good clean shot at it.

Since the seventeenth century, the English pointer has been bred for pointing game and it was great to see Bud at work, running through the forest in front of us sniffing for pheasant but never getting so far ahead that the bird would be out of range. When pointers find a bird, they freeze, pointing their bodies in the direction of where the bird is hiding. This is the hunter's cue to move into a good shooting position. Eventually the dog runs towards the bird, flushing it into the air for the shooter to get a shot.

That's how it's meant to happen, but in a broken forest there are trees and lots of other obstacles that make it difficult to get a decent clean shot at a fast-flying pheasant.

The hunters spent hours following scrubby creeks and streams, climbing fences, bashing through bush — all the time watching Bud's body language for any sign of prey. He was head down, running a zigzag course in front of them. Then he froze. He was 20 metres in front, quivering in anticipation.

'Bill and I stood trying to make out what it was. We didn't have to wait long. Bud flushed the bush, but much to Bill's disgust, out came a wild turkey,' recalled Steve.

Bill cussed at Bud, but knew the dog was getting frustrated at the lack of birds. He explained that Bud could easily tell the difference between a turkey and a pheasant and normally wouldn't waste time chasing wild turkeys.

However, only a couple of hundred metres further down the gully Bud started to get excited again. Bill gave Steve a 'something's up' look as he loaded his gun. He was moving forward into a clearer position when they heard a sudden flap of wings. Bill had time to raise his gun but the cock pheasant was flying through the pines at good speed. Though he got one shot off, the bird had gone too far and was too fast. 'Blow it!' Bill muttered under his breath. 'That's hunting for you.'

At least they had a beautiful walk in the bush and an insurance policy called Al, and as Bill said on the long walk back to the car, 'If he can't get one at the preserve, there's something wrong with him!'

BLACK GOLD

Al had a day to spare before he could join the shoot on the preserve, so while Steve was out in the wild with Bill, he visited one of the few truffières, or commercial truffle-growing enterprises, in the country.

Considered by some as the food of kings, truffles are one of the most mysterious and expensive foods in the world, fetching as much as $3000 per kilo on the New Zealand market.

For hundreds of years the Périgord black truffle was only found in the wild oak forests of western Europe, but more recently a handful of New Zealanders have begun to successfully grow them here. The first truffière was established in New Zealand in 1987 and the first recorded truffle was harvested in 1993.

Notoriously difficult to cultivate, the truffle is a fungus that forms a symbiotic relationship with the roots of mainly oak and hazelnut trees. It produces a fruiting body that grows underground and looks a bit like a small mis-shapen avocado.

Bryan and Colleen Bassett have a black Perigord truffière near Opotiki. When Al arrived they took him to a small fenced-off section of oak and hazelnut trees, similar to a small orchard. Although some truffles were evident from what looked like mini volcanoes on the ground surface, the Bassetts' dog Jacques was needed to unearth the hidden ripe ones. His labradoodle nose readily found black gold.

Because truffles form underground, the best way to find them is by their strong aroma. In Europe they use pigs to sniff them out but Colleen and Brian use their dog Jacques. He was led under the trees and it wasn't long before he was scratching at the dirt.

Jacques was pulled off before he got too close to the truffle and Colleen carefully continued to dig with a shoe horn, eventually revealing a truffle roughly the size of a golf ball. The perfume was overwhelming — musty, slightly nutty, woody, mushroomy, with a slight sweetness. Some say it's a very earthy or autumnal smell. Whatever it is, it's unique.

sniffing truffles

finally al earns the right to shoot

al bill grace and logie

preparing the pheasant

adding grated truffle

dinner at bill and grace's

THE PHEASANT PRESERVE AT TITOKI

Al: I was completely blown away by the speed of these birds. They appeared very high overhead at lightning speed and Liz was in her element dropping them left, right and centre.

It was a beautiful dawn when Al arrived at Titoki, where organised shoots are held every Saturday during the winter months. Having converted their farm into a pheasant preserve over a decade ago, John and Liz Wells run what's considered to be one of the best preserves in the country.

Preserves are about shooting pheasants rather than hunting them and if you're a good shot, you'll get the opportunity to drop a lot of them. The 12 shoot days each year are highly orchestrated affairs. Eight 'shooters' or 'guns' each pay handsomely for the right to shoot. The 50-odd other people are there to help make it happen. Many come as volunteers to give their gun dogs some experience and others are there to enjoy the atmosphere of a shoot day.

With punters paying six grand for the day's shooting, Al knew he needed to be creative if he was going to get a chance to shoot. He started by making some pheasant breast sandwiches for people as they arrived. Cooked on the barbecue, the breasts are sliced thinly and stuffed between two slices of white bread, then finished with tomato relish and Liz's Titoki mayonnaise.

As more people arrived, the buzz and excitement of the shoot day increased. Dogs of every shape and size were strutting their stuff and leaving their mark on the tyres of the Land Rovers, Range Rovers and countless other four-wheel-drives. There were tweeds and guns, friends reuniting and folk meeting for the first time — a heady mix of adrenalin and anticipation.

Following a sharp blow of the horn, John briefed everyone on the day's activities and the rules of the shoot. With six drives or shoots, the 'guns' are allowed a tally of 400 birds for the day and once that figure has been reached they have to start paying for each extra bird that is shot. The day is based on a traditional English shoot, but has a more egalitarian Kiwi approach with less of a divide between the 'shooters' and the rest. At the end of the day everyone gets to take home a share of the pheasants, but at this stage in the proceedings all Al could think of was how he was actually going to get the chance to shoot a pheasant himself.

LIZ'S TITOKI MAYONNAISE

INGREDIENTS

1 tin Highlander sweetened
   condensed milk
2 egg yolks
1 large teaspoon mustard powder
1 cup malt vinegar

1 cup canola oil
1 teaspoon salt
1 teaspoon pepper
¼ teaspoon wasabi paste or
   horseradish (optional)

METHOD

Place all the ingredients into a food blender and blend for 2 minutes. Place in jar in fridge to set.

HUNTING ON SPEED

Liz and John are brilliant hosts and certainly know how to run a great day's shooting. Liz, a mad-keen shooter, grabbed a gun and decided to show Al the ropes on the first of the six drives held throughout the day. Each drive is carried out at a different area of the preserve where the plump, grain-fed pheasants will be flushed out of the bushes to fly high over the heads of the shooters.

Once everyone is in place, a command is relayed by walkie-talkie to the line of 'beaters' positioned on the hill above and they start moving forward with their dogs flushing the pheasants.

The pheasants lived up to every bit of their reputations for rapid flight and being a sporting target as Al watched Liz line up her first shot of the day.

The first drive provided Al with a good taste of what a shoot is all about, but there was no gun on offer and plenty of spadework to be done, starting with retrieving.

Fetchers and their dogs — many of them cocker spaniels that are specifically bred for this role — drive from all over the North Island to be present on shoot days. The dogs can get more retrieves in one day at Titoki than they would all season in the wild, so it's an opportunity to get the dogs some valuable experience.

After the first two drives, morning tea was served, with an elaborate selection of cakes and savouries, fresh tea and coffee. It was a chance to swap stories and recall the morning's shoot. People talked about the birds they missed, the ones they got and the tally so far. There was a great sense of occasion, set amongst beautiful surroundings.

Titoki is a magnificent property. Once a thriving sheep and beef farm, the transition to a preserve has seen huge areas of land being planted back to native forest and wetlands. Over the years, John and Liz have planted thousands of native trees and can be very proud of their carbon footprint. Preserves also play a useful role helping to maintain wild pheasant stocks. Titoki releases thousands of birds every year, many of which escape to the wild

Titoki preserve even has an English gamekeeper, Richard Minney. It's his job to look after the birds from the day they arrive right through to shoot day. Richard studied gamekeeping at university in England where keeping game for shoots has been practised for hundreds of years.

AL GETS HIS BAG

Al had been working hard to impress John Wells. At lunchtime he had been head carver for the beautiful roast of pork. He'd fetched in the morning and for the second-to-last shoot of the day he teamed up with John's son Peter to do some beating. Sporting a bright orange safety vest and safety glasses, in a coordinated line with the other beaters he had run down the hill madly shouting, waving and flushing pheasants out onto the guns below. 'It was actually great fun — once I got used to the idea that there was a chance I

PHEASANTS

Pheasants are thought to have been introduced to New Zealand as early as the 1840s. Their striking plumage and high-yielding superb eating qualities make them one of New Zealand's most sought-after game birds.

The pheasants seen in the wild are ringneck pheasants and are a hybrid of three distinct breeds: the blackneck pheasant imported in 1853 by Henry Watson; the Chinese ringneck pheasant from Shanghai; and the large Mongolian pheasant introduced in 1914 by acclimatisation societies.

At first the pheasant population thrived and grew, with the first official shooting of pheasants being approved by the acclimatisation societies as early as 1866. However, within the space of 20 years, the pheasant population is said to have declined dramatically.

The New Zealand hunting season is set by the Fish and Game Council and runs from the first weekend of May through until about mid-August each year, but this can vary slightly from region to region. It is illegal to shoot female pheasants in the wild.

Pheasants have a magnificent plumage. Hen feathers are brown, beige and black and they have cream-coloured throats. The cocks have a white ring around their neck, hence the common name ringneck.

A SHORT HISTORY OF THIS REGION

The district is located on the volcanic plateau that was active for millennia and continues to be active with hot springs. Most of the lakes in the district are craters formed by ancient explosions, but Lake Rotorua is a shallow caldera that slumped after volcanic activity emptied the magma chamber beneath. Mount Ngongotaha and Mokoia Island were also formed after this collapse, which occurred about 100,000 years ago.

Rotorua district has a population of 68,360. Most people live in Rotorua city (52,000 people), with the rest in smaller townships and rural areas.

According to legend, the navigator priest Ngatoroirangi who first came here on the Arawa canoe, 'drew fire to warm himself on the frozen slopes of Tongariro'.

In 1843 Seymour Mills Spencer established a Christian mission on Tauraroa on the shores of Lake Tarawera.

Early visitors spread word of the wonders of this geothermal area and the pink and white terraces became famous. By 1860 there was a thriving tourism industry there.

The pink and white terraces were formed by the silica-rich waters of Lake Rotomahana being warmed by the magma below. The larger white terraces covered nearly three hectares, descending 30 metres. The smaller pink terraces were lower down, where three-metre basins filled with hot water made superb bathing holes.

New Zealand's greatest natural disaster occurred on the night of 10 June 1886, when eruptions from Tarawera's three peaks reached thousands of metres into the sky. The basalt magma mixed with the hydrothermal system, blew out the bed of Lake Rotomahana, also destroying the pink and white terraces. Two villages, Te Ariki and Moura, were also buried that night. Today the remains make up the tourist destination called the Buried Village. It's estimated that more than 120 people died that night.

Tourism is a major source of employment in this area, along with forestry, manufacturing and retail.

1. Logie and Bill hunting around here
2. Titoki phesant preserve here
3. Roadside Jerusalem artichokes

Tauranga

Te Puke

Whakatane

Kawerau

Rotorua

could take a hit with a stray shot at any stage,' said Al.

After the shoot and feeling like he had completed his apprenticeship, Al approached Liz and John who generously offered him a gun for the last drive of the day.

By the time he got into position the adrenalin was pumping. Then the first of the birds started coming over the top and he was into it, having a crack at anything that came his way and experiencing first-hand how difficult these birds are to hit. Luckily, he managed to bag a couple of handsome pheasants.

Ideally, pheasants, like a lot of game meats, need to be hung for a few days to relax the muscles and to allow the enzymes to start to break down any toughness in the meat, so at the end of the shoot Al swapped his pheasants for two that had already been hung and were ready to cook.

Al: For anyone who's got six grand to spare — yes, it's expensive — it's a brilliant day out and good value when you realise what's involved. It's like hunting on speed!

ROADSIDE DELI

Even though Steve didn't get a pheasant in the wild, there was no need to come back empty-handed. In rural New Zealand there's always something to be found, if you use a little bit of thought and keep your eyes open.

After a tip-off from a local, Steve headed to a busy stretch of highway just north of Te Puke where, beside a kilometre-long stretch of road, there was an amazing patch of Jerusalem artichokes.

A great winter vegetable, the Jerusalem artichoke is a type of sunflower, native to North America, which grows easily in New Zealand. The tuber, the edible part, is knobbly in shape yet has a lovely smooth texture when peeled, boiled and blended. Jerusalem artichokes have a wonderful earthy flavour and are especially excellent for mashing, roasting and puréeing. They were just what we needed to complement the confit of pheasant.

DINNER FIT FOR A KING

Pheasants are great eating. Similar to chicken, they have a little more texture and a lot more flavour. This is especially true of pheasants from a preserve that have been fed three square meals a day. For one shot, you get a lot of bird.

After plucking and cleaning the bird, we were ready to prepare our feast in Grace's meticulously spotless kitchen, which we were about to ruin!

Like many people around the country, particularly of Grace and Bill's generation, it's common to see small backyard fruit and vege gardens, growing old favourites, such as rhubarb, curly leafed parsley and lemons. Grace had a great patch of silver beet ready for the taking. It's a highly underrated vegetable and its robust leaves would bring a good texture and foil to the dish we were planning.

It was wonderful to cook this sophisticated dish, using all the ingredients we'd gathered from the region including Grace's garden, and to enjoy it with Bill and Grace in their welcoming home.

PAN-SEARED PHEASANT BREAST WITH CONFIT LEG, JERUSALEM ARTICHOKE PURÉE AND TRUFFLE OIL By Al Brown

This dish is about as close as you'll get to what we would serve at Logan Brown. It's a sophisticated and refined autumnal dish with incredible flavour combinations and textures — it's food fit for a king or queen.

The term confit refers to an old method of preserving, where the meat is cooked slowly in fat, usually duck fat, cooled and then set in the fat.

Truffles are a bit of a stretch, but can be substituted with any form of mushroom that's available.

Serves 4 as a main.

STEP 1. PHEASANT LEG CONFIT

INGREDIENTS
4 pheasant legs
1 teaspoon minced garlic
1 teaspoon minced juniper berries
1 tablespoon fresh thyme, finely chopped
1 bay leaf, crushed
1 tablespoon Maldon salt
¼ teaspoon freshly ground black pepper
4 cups rendered duck fat

METHOD
Place the pheasant legs in an ovenproof dish. Make sure they fit snugly. Now add the garlic, juniper, thyme, bay leaf, salt and pepper to the dish and rub thoroughly over the pheasant legs. Cover with cling film and marinate in the fridge for at least two days.

To cook, take the duck fat and melt in a saucepan. Pour over the legs, cover with foil and place in a preheated oven at 120–130°C. Check the pheasant legs after 2–3 hours. They are ready when the meat is tender and coming away from the bone with ease. Leave in the duck fat and cool to room temperature. Refrigerate until required. Submerged in the fat the pheasant legs will last for at least two months.

STEP 2. JERUSALEM ARTICHOKE PURÉE

INGREDIENTS

800 g peeled Jerusalem artichokes, roughly chopped
1½ cups cream
salt and pepper

METHOD

Place the peeled artichokes in a suitable-sized saucepan. Cover with cold water and a pinch of salt. Place on the heat, bring up to the boil then simmer for about 20 minutes until soft. Strain off the water and add the cream. Place back on low heat and reduce the cream by half. Pour the artichokes and cream mixture into a liquidiser or similar and purée until super smooth. Season with salt and pepper to taste. When cool, refrigerate until required.

STEP 3. COOKING, PLATING AND SERVING

INGREDIENTS

4 confit pheasant legs
50 g fresh truffles
4 pheasant breasts
1 bunch silver beet, stalks removed, roughly chopped
knob of butter
Jerusalem artichoke purée
1 cup demi-glaze or gravy
truffle oil or porcini oil to garnish

METHOD

Place a saucepan of salted water on the heat and bring up to the boil for the silver beet. Turn on the oven to 180°C. Likewise place the demi-glaze or gravy in a small pot and place on low heat.

Remove the confit legs from the duck fat. Heat up a skillet or sauté pan to medium-high heat. Once hot, place the legs skin side down in the pan and cook for 1 to 2 minutes until the skin is golden. Remove and place in an ovenproof dish and keep warm.

If you have fresh truffles, shave eight thin slices and carefully place two between the skin and flesh of each pheasant breast. Heat a skillet or frying pan to medium-high and season the breasts and place skin-side down in the pan.

Drop the silver beet into the boiling water and start heating up the artichoke purée in the microwave or in a pot over low heat. Place the confit legs in the oven.

Cook each breast for a couple of minutes on either side until medium. Remove and rest in a warm place for at least 5 minutes. Drain cooked silver beet and season with salt and pepper and a knob of butter.

To serve, place four warmed plates on the bench. Spoon about half a cup of artichoke purée into the centre of each plate and top with some silver beet.

Slice the breasts and arrange on each plate. Place a confit leg on each plate and pour around some gravy. Drizzle a little truffle or porcini oil over and around each plate and finally, if you have a fresh truffle, grate a little over each dish. Serve pronto.

STEVE'S WINE RECOMMENDATIONS

Mills Reef Cabernet Sauvignon Merlot

This style of wine is quite big with aggressive tannins, but this particular wine has quite soft tannins, making it a good match for the relatively mild pheasant meat. The wine has nice savoury characteristics to pick up on the dish's mushroomy notes and it also has good ripe fruit to complement the game.

There are people who object to the concept of preserves, but we think they have their place. At Titoki, Liz and John Wells are doing a lot of great things to enrich the region by replanting natives and bringing back wetlands and, importantly, seeding pheasants in the wild. Like any free-range animal the pheasants lead a natural life in perfect conditions until they are shot. And the birds are dispatched as quickly and humanely as possible.

If reincarnated we would certainly rather come back as majestic pheasants with the run of a preserve than as battery hens.

Al: Steve and I get as much pleasure out of gathering ingredients, as we do from hunting. Having the opportunity to gather this incredible produce was a highlight. To uncover these truffles and handle them straight from the soil was amazing, especially knowing how well they would complement the pheasant in our dish.

FLOUNDER ON
KAWHIA HARBOUR

FLOUNDERING AROUND IN KAWHIA

Pan-fried flounder, a squeeze of lemon, chips and iceberg lettuce with condensed milk mayonnaise, is a Kiwi family favourite that evokes many happy childhood memories. As we were heading into Kawhia, famous for its flounder, our mouths were drooling at the thought of indulging in that sweet-tasting, succulent, flat fish.

As we drove around Kawhia Harbour we were looking forward to meeting a few locals and learning how they catch and cook flounder. Then, with a bit of luck, we hoped to catch a few for ourselves before preparing our own dish of flounder and local pipis.

Situated in the North Island, Kawhia is the largest of three harbours on the Waikato's west coast. The spiritual home of the Tainui people, this region has been cherished for its abundant seafood and temperate climate for hundreds of years.

For years we had flown over this part of the country and often noticed the great expanse of harbour from the window. It was great to finally be seeing it from ground level. We could tell we were getting close. We were getting friendly waves from on-coming cars — the lazy finger off the steering wheel, the thumbs up or the nod of acknowledgement commonly shared in rural areas and small communities.

As we came down the final hill the expanse of the harbour opened up and all we could see for miles was mudflats. No doubt about it, we were in flounder country. We turned right and followed the northern side of the harbour to the tiny village of Kawhia, which looks like one of those towns that was built to grow, but somehow never did — and a good thing that is, too. The few biggish buildings have nice solid structures, built at a time when the effort was put in to make places that would last.

With a population of some 650, it's got that end-of-the-road kind of feel, where the wharf is often busier than the main street. That's how the locals like it.

THE HAPPY FLOUNDER

Like most small villages in New Zealand, Kawhia has a pub, a dairy, a petrol station and a fish 'n' chip shop.

Kawhia's fish 'n' chip shop, The Happy Flounder, looked like the obvious place to go for a first taste of the region and to find out who's who in the floundering business.

We wandered in and met the owner of the shop Greg Taylor, a giant of a man with a massive beard to match! He looked like a roadie for ZZ Top and although we were slightly intimidated by his staunch demeanour he turned out to be a top bloke with a wicked sense of humour.

It was great to meet Greg, but we weren't so lucky on the flounder front. He'd sold out for the day, but on the menu there was lemon fish freshly caught from the harbour. Lemon fish or rig is actually a small shark and is one of the more common fish used in fish 'n' chip shops around the country. Its moist flesh, lack of bones and big flakes make it perfect for deep frying.

Greg's light batter, clean oil and fresh fish are the essential ingredients for a top-notch feed of shark and taties. The fish, encased in a thin layer of crunchy batter, was magnificent. The chips were incredible too. As all good fish 'n' chip connoisseurs know, the perfect chip is hand cut just like Greg's.

It's not often that you can sit beside a harbour and enjoy seafood that fresh. Without a doubt, these were the most awesome fish and chips we'd ever eaten. We'd happily take a two-hour drive off the beaten track just to experience this culinary delight once more.

GREG TAYLOR'S FISH BATTER

Greg's light batter, clean oil and fresh fish are the essential ingredients for a top-notch feed of shark and taties.

Make a very light batter mix from flour and water, so that it's almost water again, and then add a dash of baking soda. In the shop they make it with three good cups of flour, one beer jug of water, plus about a quarter of a teaspoon of baking soda. The secret is to use ice-cold water so that when the batter hits the vat it fluffs up well. It is also important to coat whatever is being fried in seasoned flour before battering it.

Being the only fast food available in New Zealand for many years, fish 'n' chips are a huge part of New Zealand culture. For us and most Kiwis our generation, it was our first experience of food cooked by someone else. Wrapped in yesterday's newspaper, it represented a bundle of happiness, the aroma hitting you as soon as the pack was ripped open. Wattie's tomato sauce and a wedge of lemon, if you're lucky, are all the condiments you need.

'Tomato sauce or ketchup with fish 'n' chips is one of the greatest flavour combinations I can think of,' said Al. 'The reason for its popularity is that the vinegar in the sauce cuts through the fat and the sweetness balances out the salt. Wine match — forget it! Everyone knows that Fanta, Coke or L&P go the best.'

We'd had a great taste of what the harbour can offer but we weren't here just for the fish 'n' chips. It was flounder we were after.

FISHING WITH GREG'S OLD MAN ON KAWHIA HARBOUR

We quickly figured out that if the fish 'n' chip shop was out of flounder, someone would be going out to catch some, and since Kawhia is such a small town it didn't take us long to find out who that person was — the Happy Flounder owner's old man, Graham Taylor. The spitting image of Greg and a full-time fisherman, Graham supplies his son's shop with fresh flounder and other seafood most days.

We met Graham and his wife Lorraine as they were preparing to go for a fish. After sizing up the boat, which was more aptly described as a dinghy, we figured Steve had a better chance of keeping it afloat, so he went fishing, while Al went to explore more of Kawhia.

Kawhia's flounder has provided Graham and Lorraine with a livelihood for over 25 years and they have a fantastic set-up. Their home is directly across the road from the beach and, more conveniently, the boat ramp. Parked outside the front door is an old, orange Nuffield tractor, with trailer in tow — always ready to launch or retrieve the boat. Attached to the front of Graham and Lorraine's house is a large lean-to. It's a perfect place to sit, watch the tides and check water conditions over a cuppa, or maybe the odd cold beer.

Graham's boat *Manana II* is a small, flat-bottomed wooden dinghy, which is definitely not a pleasure craft. It's been designed and built specifically to work on this shallow estuary. The flat bottom gives it stability allowing it to

FLOUNDER

Flounder are bottom feeders that swim flat. Their eyes are on the tops of their heads and their neutral colours blend in with the sea floor.

All flatfish, including flounder, halibut, sole, brill and turbot are good eating with moist, sweet-tasting flesh that can probably be partly attributed to their diet of crabs and molluscs. Diners all over the globe will pay astronomical prices for flatfish.

Flounder or patiki have always been a popular source of food for Maori as they were abundant and easily caught by spearing and could be dried as a food source for winter.

In New Zealand, flounder was a mainstay on restaurant menus in the 1970s. Since then, due to other species becoming available and a preference for fillets of fish rather than having to deal with bones, flounder has fallen from favour. Recently, however, they've made a bit of a comeback as, like anything cooked on the bone, they have a great flavour.

There are 13 known species of flatfish in New Zealand: yellowbelly, sand, black and green flounder; New Zealand sole; lemon sole; brill; and turbot. Size limits for most species are 25 cm.

Commercial fishing of these species is mainly by inshore bottom trawling, with some caught by set nets and drag-nets.

slide up and down the mud banks when Graham sets his nets. By the time he and Steve launched the boat, the wind had dropped and they were setting out over the still, glassy waters of the harbour.

Kawhia Harbour is an ancient river valley that was drowned as sea levels rose. Today five rivers flow into the estuary creating a maze of channels, which, when hidden by the high tide, make for some tricky navigating. Graham's local knowledge along with some hands-on depth-sounding (with an oar) kept them off the bottom and got them to the sandbank they were heading for. Once there, setting the net was relatively straightforward.

Graham carefully anchored one end of the net, then rowed out across the estuary letting the net out as he went. When it was fully run out, he anchored the other end. Sinkers on the bottom of the line and floaters on top keep the net upright. As the tide floods in flounder moving up the harbour to feed are caught. Flounder aren't the only fish you'll find in this bountiful harbour — there's also mullet, kahawai, rig, snapper, gurnard, trevally and the odd kingfish. At low tide cockles, pipis and mussels can also be found.

With the net set, and a few hours to kill, Graham took Steve to see the sights of Kawhia Harbour, including some spectacular pancake rocks. Formed thousands of years ago by sediment being laid down on the ocean floor, the rocks were then thrust up and exposed to wind and rain. The soft bit between the layers eroded faster than the hard sediment leaving the impression of a stack of pancakes.

After checking out the rocks, Graham and Steve headed back to the net to find a couple of dozen magnificent yellowbelly flounders. It was a small catch by the usual standards, but as Graham said, 'They're fresh!'

With the tide fully in, the return trip was a lot quicker. Gutting the fish, Steve was interested to see the large number of crabs they had been feeding on. Once the flounder were dressed — skinned and boned —Lorraine had to do the paperwork involved in a small fishing business, including MoF forms recording the weight of fish as well as transfer documents for any fish on-sold, both to The Happy Flounder and through their roadside caravan.

LORRAINE'S FLOUNDER

Lorraine cooks her flounder simply and unadorned, to make the most of the freshness and moistness of this beautiful, delicately flavoured fish.

INGREDIENTS
whole flounder
flour
dripping

METHOD
Wash and dry the whole gutted flounder. Dust lightly with flour. Heat a frying pan until fairly hot and add some dripping. Cook the flounder approximately 5 minutes until the flesh is milky white. Turn and cook on the other side.

HOME OF THE TAINUI PEOPLE

The people of the Tainui waka first came to Kawhia Harbour around 800 years ago and, ever since, the place has been of great importance to the people of Tainui as this poem often heard on Tainui marae shows:

Kawhia moana
Kawhia kai
Kawhia tangata

Kawhia the waters
Kawhia the sustenance
Kawhia the people

We visited the Maketu Marae with Hone Rangawhenua who showed us the two stones marking the place where the waka is buried and then regaled us with stories of the Tainui people, their history and their mythology. 'If you touch those stones you can feel our people paddling their waka,' Hone told us as he imitated the warriors' paddling. We felt slightly intimidated by Hone's full-on, animated style of storytelling but, at the same time, we were spellbound by his antics and were keen to hear how the Maori saw this beautiful harbour that they named after its bountiful seafood.

Kawhia's rich waters were a strong enticement for the first settlers of the Tainui canoe and for hundreds of years the people living around this harbour harvested everything they needed from the land and the sea. Flounder or patiki was a major source of food. The diamond motif found in the artwork and weaving of the Tainui is a symbol for the flounder and represents abundance and the ability to provide food.

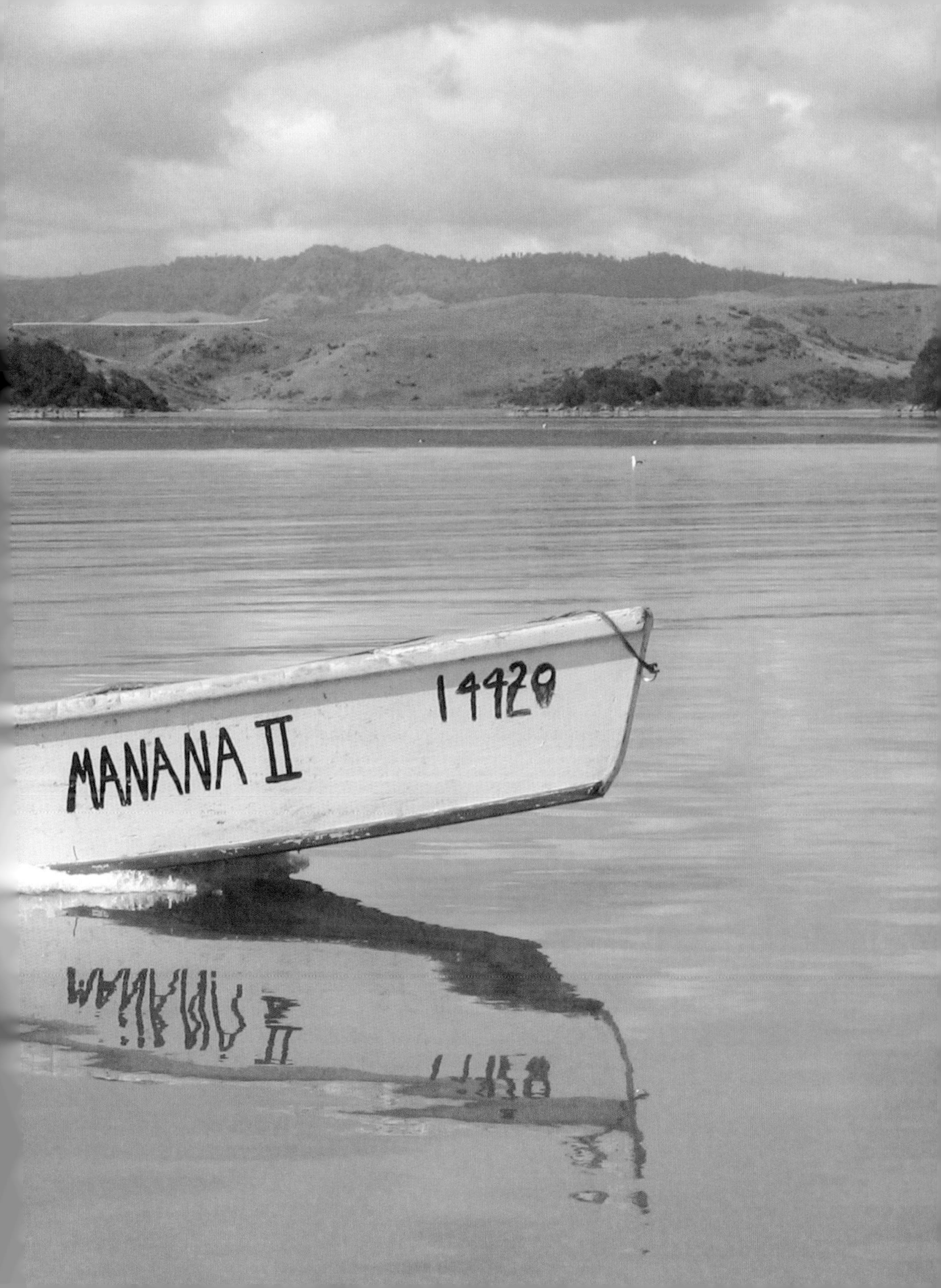
14420
MANANA II

CAROLINE'S STORY

Al: To listen to her cries in Maori as we came into the inlet was an incredibly powerful moment. As usual, I felt hopelessly inadequate in my lack of te reo and even though I didn't understand the words, the emotion and the significance of the moment was certainly not lost on me.

While Steve was out fishing with Graham, Al met up with Caroline Puke, a local Tainui woman who has a strong connection to flounder. Caroline grew up with her grandparents in an ancient cave across the harbour at Rakaunui Inlet. She and Al travelled there by boat and as they neared the cave Caroline stood and called to her ancestors. It was an awe-inspiring welcome to the place where she had spent a large part of her childhood.

At the cave she explained what her childhood had been like — mattresses of fern, sacks for warmth, drying and preserving fish and living off the bountiful kaimoana, and flounder for breakfast, lunch and tea!

It was hard to imagine life in such a harsh environment and even though the cave provided natural shelter, the long, cold, wet, winter months would have been challenging times indeed.

SPEARING FLOUNDER AT AOTEA

Spearing at night is another way to gather flounder and Al was keen to find out a bit more about it. Just over the hill from Kawhia Harbour is the smaller Aotea Harbour, where Davis Apiti spends a bit of time gathering flounder on the mud flats.

'Flounder have played a big part in our history and resource-wise that's why we're located here,' Davis told Al. 'We've been here for 700 years and it's kept us here and sustained us for that long. I'm the 34th generation, so that's not bad.'

Of the Ngati Te Wehi hapu and as a kaitiaki or guardian of his hapu's traditions, Davis is struggling to protect the resources in this region, particularly the Maui dolphin, which is unique to this part of the world. He is proactively involved in raising awareness of the risks to this critically endangered species. There are estimated to be less than 100 Maui dolphins left. Sharks are its natural predators but gill-netting has been largely blamed for the critical decline in numbers in recent years.

Flounder still feed Davis's family and night spearing is his favourite way of catching them. He took Al out with his children, Jasmine and Jessie.

They donned miners' lights and walked through, at times, knee-deep water searching for flounder. Davis also carried a strong torch attached to the end of a long pole, moving the light backwards and forwards just under the surface of the water so that he could spot these well-camouflaged fish. They covered a huge distance before eventually spotting one. Davis speared the flounder through the head and put it in an old sack-cloth bag.

Having seen flounder numbers drop dramatically over the years, Davis is concerned that the resource is looked after so that his children will be able to fish like this when they grow up. 'We've walked quite a distance,' he said. 'When I was younger you'd walk a hundred metres. You don't need to get carried away and take sacks and sacks and deplete the resource, just take what you need and be happy with that.'

graham and his wife lorraine

setting the net

night spearing

john and caroline puke

AOTEA PATIKI WITH ASIAN SAUCE

Davis is not only expert at floundering but he's pretty handy in the kitchen too. His flounder recipe is a blend of his Maori and his wife Leanne's Asian cultures, using a Chinese-style sauce of ginger, garlic and soy sauce. It is best served with a collection of home-grown, traditional Maori veges, such as kumara and wino wino leaves from the kamo kamo plant. It has simple, sweet, clean flavours and uses readily available ingredients from the kitchen and Aotea Harbour.

INGREDIENTS
fresh flounder, gutted and tail cut off
flour
salt (optional)
oil
1 bunch spring onions, finely chopped
1 tablespoon grated ginger
3 cloves garlic, finely sliced
½ cup dark soy sauce
3 tablespoons brown sugar (vary according to taste)

METHOD
Lightly coat the flounder with flour and salt, if using. Heat a generous amount of oil in a wok over a high heat and cook the flounder on both sides. Remove flounder when cooked (the meat should be white and peel easily off the bone).

Reserve the oil and clean the wok. Pour the oil back into the wok and cook the spring onion until soft then add ginger and garlic. Pour in the soy sauce and heat through. Add brown sugar to taste, enough to caramelise the sauce.

Pour sauce over the flounder and serve immediately.

A SHORT HISTORY OF THIS REGION

The great waka *Tainui* arrived with the first Maori people about 800 years ago.

In 1770 James Cook passed Kawhia in the *Endeavour*, naming Albatross Point and Gannet Island.

Pakeha first traded with Maori here in 1825 when Captain Amos Kent visited Kawhia for a cargo of flax. He returned and opened Kawhia's first trading post.

The Waikato land wars began in 1863, and in 1880 the government bought 40 acres (16 hectares) to survey as Kawhia township. The Kawhia Wharf was opened in 1901.

Te Rauparaha, one of New Zealand's most well-known tribal warriors and leader of Ngati Toa was born in this region in 1768. Both of his parents were descended from Tainui and, although not of highest rank, he rose to leadership because of his aggressive defence of the tribe and his great skill as a fighter. Based at Te Totara Pa at the southern end of Kawhia Harbour, Ngati Toa was eventually forced out as a result of war with Waikato tribes over fertile land in the region. After that Te Rauparaha took his tribe from Kawhia to fight and conquer other territories, including Taranaki and Kapiti. He lived out the remainder of his life in Otaki, where he died in 1849.

Te Papatapu

Makomako

Aotea Harbour

4

1

31

Kawhia

2

Kawhia Harbour

Rakaunui

3

1. Greg's fish and chip shop
2. Graham and Logie fish here
3. Cave where Caroline Puke lived as a child
4. Brownie and Denis go night spearing here

GATHERING OUR OWN PIPIS AND FLOUNDER

The locals gave us some great tips on floundering and it was about time we caught our own. But before we did, we wanted to gather some pipis for a simple dish to go with it.

We managed to score a quad bike and were pointed in the general direction of the pipi bed. On a wing and a prayer we managed to stumble over a small patch after digging our toes down through the sand in waist-deep water — the action commonly called the 'pipi shuffle'.

Pipis are burrowing shellfish found near fast-flowing channels. They filter the nutrients from the sea water and, in turn, become food for a variety of fish and bird life. As filter feeders pipis need to be placed in a bucket of sea water over one full tide to enable the sand to be purged, before they are ready to eat.

While the pipis were left soaking in the salt water, we borrowed an old net from Graham who pointed us in the vague direction of a mud flat on the edge of town where we could try dragging flounder by ourselves. It was great to have experienced the locals' method of catching flounder, but we wanted to have a go at dragnetting — the way we'd done it as kids holidaying on the Kapiti and Wairarapa coasts.

Like all forms of hunting and gathering, it's the anticipation of the catch (and the eating that follows) that is so exhilarating and dragging that net across the tide gave us that same thrill.

The net was about 30 metres long and 1 metre high, with an old oar attached to each end for holding and dragging it through the water. The key to success is for someone to keep one end anchored — Al's job — while the other person — Steve — drags the net through the water, always ensuring it is in contact with the sandy sea floor so the flounder can't escape underneath.

The first drag across the water yielded just one yellowbelly, but that was enough to keep the motivation levels high. 'That's a lot of graft for one flounder,' said Al. Another couple of runs and we had three yellowbellies, exactly what we needed for our main dish.

We found a wicked spot to cook our dish down at the Kawhia camping ground. It had an outdoor plumbed-in sink and bench area, designed for campers to do what we were doing — gutting and preparing fish for eating.

As usual it was a typically simple dish, using the freshest of ingredients. It goes back to being asked, as a chef, what's the best food we've ever eaten. For us, it's favourite moments like these, two great mates, looking out onto the harbour, cooking pipis in wine with a beautiful fresh flounder cooked simply in a skillet, accompanied by a delicious white wine. That beats any five-star Michelin restaurant in France every time.

We used to wonder why anyone would want to live next to mud flats, but coming here and watching the tides come and go, it's kind of peaceful. We left Kawhia and Aotea with an appreciation of the simple pleasures of life and and a new understanding of the delicate balance between the need to fish for a living and managing our seafood resource for future generations.

SAUTÉED FLOUNDER WITH FRESH PIPIS IN WHITE WINE, HERBS AND GARLIC

There's something special about eating two different sorts of seafood together. This is a tactile dish with lots of rolling up of sleeves and picking out pipis from the shell and finding the lovely crunchy bits on the edge of the flounder. Everyone gets a whole flounder to themselves and there's also something about a plate of pipis when they've just opened out, like a jewel inside each shell. The broth that remains is a pure shot of the sea — butter, garlic and a hit of the surf.

Serves 8 as a main.

STEP 1. FRESH PIPIS IN WHITE WINE

INGREDIENTS

pipis, purged in salt water for at least 12 hours (allow 30–40 per serve)

1½ cups white wine

2 cups chicken stock

½ tablespoon garlic

100 g butter

¼ cup fresh basil

3 tablespoons fresh tarragon

METHOD

Place the pipis, wine, chicken stock, garlic and butter in a large saucepan and cover with a lid. Place the saucepan over a high heat. Check after 5 to 7 minutes and if the shells are beginning to open add the fresh herbs. Place the lid back on and give them a good shake up. Cook for a couple more minutes and set aside until ready to serve.

STEP 2. SAUTÉED FLOUNDER

INGREDIENTS

8 flounder, gutted

salt and pepper to season

flour

cooking oil

butter

METHOD

To prepare the flounder, hold the tail with one hand, then take your other hand and using your thumb, carefully edge it between the dark top skin and the flesh. It should start to come away. Then holding the tail, securely pull

the skin back towards the head and remove, exposing the top fillet. To cook the flounder, heat up a skillet, frying pan or flat top to medium heat. Season the flounders with salt and pepper then dredge with flour and pat any excess off, leaving a fine layer of flour over the fish. Add cooking oil, then butter to the pan and cook each flounder until golden on each side. For a regular-sized flounder, 3 to 4 minutes on each side should be ample. Keep the flounders warm until all are cooked.

STEP 3. PLATING AND SERVING

Serve the flounder on a flat plate. Top with pipis and spoon over some broth. Have plenty of paper towels ready at the table, as extracting the pipis from their shells and removing the middle bone frame from the flounder is finger-lickin' fun. A good loaf of bread to mop up the pipi broth is a great idea!

STEVE'S WINE RECOMMENDATION

Seresin Marama Marlborough Sauvignon Blanc
Typically Marlborough Sauvignon Blancs are relatively simple, with fresh zippy fruit characters, but Seresin Marama is a more complex Sauvignon Blanc as the fruit is fermented by wild yeast in oak casks, almost like a Chardonnay. The wine is then aged on its lees or dead yeast cells, and the resulting wine has a lovely creamy texture with rich fruit flavours that complement the flounder and buttery pipi broth. The wine's crisp acidity also refreshes the palate between mouthfuls.

PADDLE CRABS
ON THE KAPITI COAST

THEY'RE TRICKY CUSTOMERS TO GET HOLD OF

Being less than an hour north of the capital, the Kapiti Coast is a well-travelled path for many Wellingtonians. There's a great sense of arrival as you pass through Pukerua Bay and the coastline opens up in front of you. There's also the formidable Kapiti Island. Formed by earthquakes 200 million years ago, it stands five kilometres off the coast of the mainland.

The Kapiti coastline is a narrow stretch of fertile land that runs between the Tararua Ranges and the sea — and the flat, sandy bottom in between this coast and Kapiti Island is an ideal home for paddle crabs, known locally as Waikanae crabs.

We were looking forward to finding some of these feisty paddlers with the help of a couple of locals who fish for them regularly, and making one of our all-time favourite dishes — crab cakes with homemade tartare sauce — to share with our friends.

Crabs aren't very popular in New Zealand probably because there's a lot of work involved in extracting the meat, but at Logan Brown we rate them pretty highly. Waikanae crabs are about as close as we can get to serving local produce and the meat is sweet. Crab cakes have become one of our signature dishes.

MATT AND NARINA'S CRAB SHED

Matt Whittaker and Narina McBeath of Waikanae Crab are true pioneers of the crabbing industry. They've been delivering a steady supply of crabs to restaurants all over the country for more than 20 years, including Logan Brown for more than a decade and, before that, Steve's first restaurant, Brer Fox Café.

When Matt and Narina first started the business, there was virtually no interest in crab meat here, but as it is such a restaurant favourite in the United States, they could see it had potential. They started off with a small 16-foot (4.9 metre) boat, selling green crabs to fish markets and Asian restaurants. It took about 10 years to build a market and at one stage they employed up to 11 people with boats working on the Kapiti Coast, Wairarapa, Wellington and in Golden Bay.

Matt and Narina converted an old dairy shed along the coast, where they process the catch before sending it around the country. They still work from the dairy shed and that's where we caught up with them, processing the day's catch. After many enjoyable phone conversations, it was fantastic to be spending time with them at last and learning about what they do.

After each morning's fishing, the crabs are taken to the shed where Narina and Matt process the meat. The crabs are killed instantly by removing their backs. Narina then briefly cooks them in boiling water and Matt extracts the flesh while it's still hot.

Like all pioneers they found what worked best by trial and error and often the simplest solutions win out. The crabs are boiled in an old fish 'n' chip fryer and a heavy rolling pin is run across the crab to push out all the meat — about one-third of a crab's weight is edible meat.

Steve: A lot of people would have said that it's too hard and too labour-intensive to process paddle crabs, and after seeing the work involved it's easy to understand why it usually sells for more than $70 a kilo.

CRABBING WITH SANJAY

Steve stayed on with Matt to go crab fishing the next day and Al went off to gather the rest of the ingredients for the crab cakes and tartare sauce.

Logan Brown is in the heart of the Cuba quarter, the last bastion of a quirky village left in Wellington, where everyone knows everyone on the street. Just down the road from Logan Brown is the restaurant's greengrocer, Sanjay Dayal, from Cuba St Fruit Mart. He had all the extra fresh ingredients needed for the dish. 'We all support each other — whether it's the local coffee roaster or where we get our hair cut — it's how we like to operate,' said Al.

Most weeks, Al drops in on Sanjay for a catch-up and to see what produce he's got. Usually it's around lunchtime. Out the back of the shop Sanjay has an electric burner and a small toastie oven. If it's Tuesday, there's usually dhal and roti and on Thursdays, Lucka's chicken curry. On very rare occasions — when the stars line up — there is Sanjay's mum Puspa's leftover crab curry.

When Al turned up looking for red onion, tarragon and herbs for his crab cakes there was no curry, but something even better was on offer — Sanjay invited Al to go crabbing and to watch Puspa make her famous curry.

They loaded a couple of crab pots into the Holden and headed out to Sanjay's secret spot in Wellington's Lyall Bay. With wetsuits on they headed down to the beach where they started baiting the pots. Sanjay reckoned crabs would go for salmon heads, but Al had his own theory, and produced a roasted chicken from the supermarket. They baited up, waded out to waist-deep water and threw their pots — competition on!

Lyall Bay is a broad, sandy-bottomed bay — an ideal habitat for paddle crabs — and that day, with minimal swell and an off-shore wind, the conditions were perfect. After a 15 minute soak, it was time to check the pots — the moment of truth had arrived. Sanjay's pot held three crabs and when Al pulled up what was left of the fatty chicken carcass there were a good dozen crabs in his pot. Another few sets and they had a good haul of crabs to take back to Puspa.

Puspa comes from a coastal Indian village where crab is considered a delicacy. We prepared the crabs for the curry by taking off the backs and breaking off the outside joints of the legs to expose as much of the crab meat as possible.

Al: I'd only tasted Puspa's crab curry twice and I was looking forward to meeting the creator of this wonderful dish. She was lovely — so at home in her kitchen and such a natural cook.

In Puspa's kitchen, spices take pride of place and she set about preparing her curry, using fresh curry leaves, her own garam masala blended from a family recipe, turmeric for colour, cumin seeds, onions, ginger and fresh chillies. The heady aromas coming out of that pot were mind blowing. The crab halves were dropped in the pot, some tamarind was added to give the curry some sourness and, lastly, Puspa added puréed fresh tomatoes. The lid was placed on the pot signifying dinner would be ready in five minutes.

We all sat outside and, right on cue, we were joined by the extended family members — they all know that when Puspa makes her crab curry, it pays to be in the vicinity.

There were bowls of curried crab on rice, poppadoms, homemade roti and lime pickle and Sanjay's 'traditional naan bread', a loaf of sliced white from the supermarket.

'From the start to the finish, this Indian-style crabbing was terrific. It was great to experience how another culture enjoys harvesting and using the fruits our wonderful country has to offer,' said Al, 'straight out of Lyall Bay and into the pot. Now that's fresh!'

Al: Sanjay tells me that there are more Indian recipes for cooking crab than there are Indians, but that his mum's dish is his favourite.

PUSPA'S CRAB CURRY

INGREDIENTS

4 tablespoons oil
1 teaspoon fenugreek seeds
2 medium onions, finely chopped
10 curry leaves
2 teaspoons ground cumin
2 teaspoons ground coriander
1 teaspoon garam masala
1 teaspoon turmeric
1 minced green chilli and 1 teaspoon chilli powder or 1½–2 teaspoons
    chilli powder
2 teaspoons crushed garlic
3 teaspoons crushed ginger
2 teaspoons salt
approximately 15 crabs
30 g tamarind soaked in 1½ cups hot water and drained or 2 teaspoons
    lemon juice
800 g fresh tomatoes, skins removed, puréed
spring onions, finely chopped
fresh coriander, roughly chopped
1 teaspoon garam masala to garnish

METHOD

Heat the oil in a large, deep saucepan. Add the fenugreek seeds and brown.
Add onion and curry leaves, then all the spices, chilli, garlic, ginger and salt.
Stir and cook gently until the onions are soft. Add crabs, stir, close the lid and
steam for several minutes, stirring several times. Add tamarind water and
bring to boil. Now add the tomatoes and simmer for 10 minutes. Garnish with
spring onions and fresh coriander and sprinkle garam masala over the top.

ABOUT PADDLE CRABS

The New Zealand paddle crab (*Ovalipes catharus*) or papaka is a sand dweller found around the coast of New Zealand.

Crabs are a favourite food of snapper and groper.

They feed at night mostly on a diet of living animal matter, including cockles, pipi and tuatua. They also cannibalise younger crabs, particularly during moulting. They will feed on dead fish too.

They are most commonly found in about 10 metres of water, but may also be found in deeper waters.

Female crabs are generally smaller than males and have a pale, greyish-brown shell with brown speckles. Males tend to be darker coloured. The carapace or shell can be up to 12 cm across for females and up to 15 cm for males.

Their distinctive, broad, paddle-shaped back legs are ideal for both swimming and digging sand.

Paddle crabs have been commercially harvested since the 1980s, mainly using baited traps and pots. They are also a common by-catch of trawling, dredging and set-netting.

FISHING FOR WAIKANAE CRABS WITH MATT

After serving Waikanae crab in the restaurant for the past 10 years, it was great for Steve to be going out with Matt to experience what crab fishing is all about.

Weather permitting, Matt goes out every day and, on occasions, twice a day. Like most fishing it requires an early start but as most fishermen would agree, that's the best time of day.

Matt's first job is to launch his boat through the surf, which is no mean feat for one bloke. With tractor and trailer he backs the boat out into the surf and he has to quickly drive off to park the tractor before the boat moves too far. When he can, Matt gets one of the locals to drive the tractor for him, so he can head straight out through the surf and start fishing.

Paddle crabs are found off sandy beaches and in harbours and estuaries throughout New Zealand. Matt fishes the length of the Kapiti Coast anywhere from just beyond the breakers out to a couple of kilometres offshore.

The crabs feed on baby flounder, molluscs, worms and shellfish, and scavenge for anything dead on the sea floor. They use their two strong claws to tear into their food, using one as a holder and the other to cut, just like scissors.

Catching paddle crabs can be difficult because they're constantly on the move as they travel in groups across the sandy sea floor searching for food. The difficult part is finding what depth they're feeding at and so the first thing Matt does is drop a few exploratory pots where he thinks they'll be.

Matt uses two types of pot — a set pot and a lift pot. The set pot is similar to a cray pot — when the crabs climb in they're trapped, so the pots can be left soaking for long periods, from two hours to overnight. The lift pots are more like square trays and because there is nothing stopping the crabs from getting out, they need to be lifted every 15 to 20 minutes.

Steve and Matt threw over a few set pots before heading to a spot just beyond the breakers to work the lift pots. Baited with fish frames and set 50 metres apart, it was a slick operation and soon 10 pots were put over the side.

After about 15 minutes they went back to the start to lift the traps. This was one of the best examples of multi tasking Steve had ever seen. Matt was monitoring the weather and sea, keeping an eye on wind shifts and other boats as he worked the winch, lifted the pots, rebaited and set the pots and drove the boat.

Lifting the pots was a full-on job and Steve was impressed with the whole operation — except for the number of crabs caught. The first 10 pots turned up only a few. Matt reckoned they were fishing at the wrong depth, so decided to up sticks and look for new grounds.

For Matt, every day on the water is different and that's what he loves about working the sea. Quite often he'll see whales and sharks and on most trips he gets a visit from his one-legged mate, a seagull called Hoppy.

al sits down to lunch with
the dayal family

puspa's crab curry

sanjay and al

crabbing with matt

narina and al

crab cakes on kapiti

His catch varies, depending on the tides, the moon and the wind, so success is never guaranteed. Sometimes his set pots are empty and the lift pots full, or vice versa. Catching crabs is as much about luck as it is about local knowledge.

Steve: The day was getting on and the bins were still empty, which was a bit of a worry, given that we were supposed to be cooking crab cakes on our return. I discovered that crabbing is a bit of a hit-and-miss affair.

BETTER LUCK HERE, MAYBE

Matt wasn't too worried about the lack of crab in the bins. He had obviously been there many times before. He headed out further to a new spot and a new depth — hopefully, to where crabs were feeding.

After setting a line of traps and letting them soak for 15 minutes he and Steve lifted the first to find a few good-sized crabs crawling over it. Usually, where you find one paddle crab, you'll find many and as they pulled each trap the numbers got progressively better. By the end of the line, the traps were looking full.

With a bin full of large paddle crabs, Matt was satisfied with the day's haul. There were even a few extra for Steve and Al to take away with them.

NATURE'S LOLLIES

Al: There's something delightful about being in an orchard in summer. As a child being able to 'pick your own' was like a dream come true — only to be followed by an almighty bellyache in the back of the station wagon on the long drive home.

After a belly full of curried crab, Al headed back up the coast making two more stops before hooking up with Steve to see how he had got on with Matt out in the boat.

First, Al picked up Narina and they headed up the road to Windsor Gardens to pick some fresh berries for dessert.

The fertile soils of the Kapiti Coast have long been known as Wellington's food basket and berries thrive in the coastal climate. The sweet juice and bright colours of berries are a device to attract birds and animals to disperse their seeds — 'nature's lollies' according to Al.

Windsor Gardens is a terrific orchard, living up to its reputation for outstanding fruit and a great variety of berries. The job was completed in less than 20 minutes and Al and Narina left with a bowl full of blueberries, raspberries, strawberries and blackberries. 'The only berry I found slightly sour for some reason was the loganberry!' said Al.

TUATARAS FROM THE RED SHED

With the greens from Sanjay and the fresh berries, there was just one thing missing — a cold beer. Tuatara Brewery, owned by husband and wife team Carl and Simone Vasta, and housed in an old red barn that looks like a shearing shed, is tucked away in the back-blocks of Waikanae. It's an award-winning brewery that's gaining a great reputation around the country. With a typical brewer's welcome, in a matter of seconds Al was handed a glass of one of the finest freshly brewed cold beers imaginable. Their Pilsner is clean and crisp with a wonderful citrus aroma and a flavour of hops that lingers nicely.

Carl and Simone are another fine example of a husband and wife team carving out a competitive business in the world of craft brewing. With no flash marketing campaigns, they're building their reputation on the taste of their product. 'Tuatara — what a great name — and I would recognise the refreshing, quenching finish to their fine Pilsner anywhere now,' said Al.

It was time for Al to head back to the crab shed to catch up with Matt and Steve.

OFF TO KAPITI ISLAND

With all the ingredients gathered, we were ready to head out to Kapiti Island on the regular ferry run from the mainland. We'd been invited by John Barrett, one of the few inhabitants of the island. John's whanau has been living there since the 1820s and these days John runs a successful eco lodge offering accommodation and meals for people wanting to stay on the island. We were looking forward to cooking crab cakes for everyone at the lodge and we were also expecting Matt and Narina to boat across and join us.

Steve: The locals tell me Kapiti has a real mystical aura about it. They say it either repels or attracts you and as we approached the island I felt what they meant. It could be the spirits of Maori warriors who died in battle, or the sun setting behind it that makes the island look dark and foreboding.

John Barrett, kaitiaki or guardian of the island, gave us a welcome off the ferry that was sincere, unfussed and with a quiet mana befitting his role. On the way to the lodge he told us about the island's new status as a sanctuary for endangered birds and how bird stocks have increased since possums and rats were eradicated in the 1990s.

We walked past takahe and weka and saw countless bellbirds, tui and kaka. It was great to see and hear the variety of bird life and it gave a good indication of what it must have been like on the mainland before rats, stoats and other predators were introduced.

John can tell you a lot about the bird life on Kapiti, and about the island's fascinating Maori history.

Al: As I pulled up to the beach, I could see that Steve had a grin from ear to ear as he stood next to a huge fish bin filled with the biggest paddle crabs I'd ever seen. He looked as if he'd just won Big Wednesday.

John Barrett: Several waves of Maori lived on the island, including Ngai Tahu and Ngati Mamoe. Te Rauparaha arrived later — he didn't get here until 1820 after defeating the people of the Kapiti Coast. He invited the whalers onto the island and married them off to Maori women of the Confederation of the Tribes to enhance the tribes' trading capabilities. Archaeologists reckon that there were 3000 people living on the island at one stage, when the island was thick with bird life and there was abundant seafood, such as paua, kina and fish nearby. I think, then, crabs would have been taken only as a third or fourth option.

Crabs might not have been the first option for the early inhabitants, but they were for us and we couldn't wait to cook some. At the lodge the modest kitchen felt as if, over the years, it had seen a lot of great food and a heap of laughter. Right outside the window the keg hangi for the evening was under way for the other guests and there was traditional steamed pudding bubbling away.

We set to preparing the dish for the evening, putting to good use some of the skills learnt earlier from Matt and Narina about the best way to extract meat from crabs. It was a great afternoon listening to stories of the island, catching up on activities of the day, plenty of cold Tuatara beers on hand and a chorus of birdsong outside.

Kapiti turned on a beautiful evening and as the sun started to set we cranked up the barbecue and sat out on the deck with John and his whanau, and Matt and Narina.

BERRIES WITH ROMANOFF SAUCE

Steve made a classic Romanoff Sauce to go with the summer berries. The recipe came from a friend who had a Cajun Creole restaurant in New Orleans. It's a cold caramel sauce made simply by whipping together brown sugar, sour cream and vanilla essence. It complements the sharpness of the berries and is brilliant as a last-minute, throw-together bach dessert.

Catching the crabs had been well worth the effort and getting the meat out of the shell was half the fun. And there was a bit of fun with the berries when the cheeky kaka decided they'd like to have some of nature's lollies. And where else but Kapiti Island would you get such colourful gate crashers?

Most chefs and restaurateurs dream of visiting the source of the special ingredients they use so that they can understand and appreciate them better. Finally meeting Matt and Narina after all these years and helping catch and process crabs was a real thrill for us.

We also felt incredibly lucky to be given the opportunity to prepare and eat our crab cakes with such hospitable folks on the resource- and history-rich Kapiti Island — it's a mighty place right on the doorstep of the capital city.

A SHORT HISTORY OF THIS REGION

Before 1822, Muaupoko iwi lived well on the region's rich marine and forest resources.

From 1822, Te Rauparaha led Ngati Toa iwi from Kawhia, escaping the musket wars of the Waikato and King Country regions, and established a fortress on Kapiti Island.

From 1825, Te Rauparaha's allies from Ngati Raukawa of Waikato and Te Ati Awa of Taranaki also migrated to the region.

From 1833, for more than a decade, shore whalers set up stations in the region.

In 1839, Bishop Octavius Hadfield established a Christian mission station at Kenakena Pa near the Waikanae River mouth and went on to build churches in Waikanae and Otaki.

From the 1850s onwards, both Maori and Pakeha established sheep farms from Paekakariki to Manawatu. Otaki and Paekakariki developed as trading centres.

In the 1880s, after the government bought Maori land along a proposed railway route, the Manawatu Railway Company built the line, which opened in 1886. Wiremu Parata gave land for the railway, moving Te Ati Awa village to the township of Parata, which is now Waikanae.

In 1897, the Kapiti Island Reserve Act designated all Crown-owned portions of the island as a reserve. Since the eradication of pests from the island in the 1990s, it has become one of New Zealand's leading bird sanctuaries.

From 1906, railway excursions from Wellington brought holidaymakers to the Kapiti coast where boarding houses and hotels flourished.

During the Second World War, the area supplied the US Marine camp at McKays Crossing and grew vegetables for the armed services.

Rapid economic and population growth occurred from 1960 to the mid-1970s, after which there was a period of slower growth. By the 1990s the population growth was amongst the highest in New Zealand and the district now has a population of over 46,000.

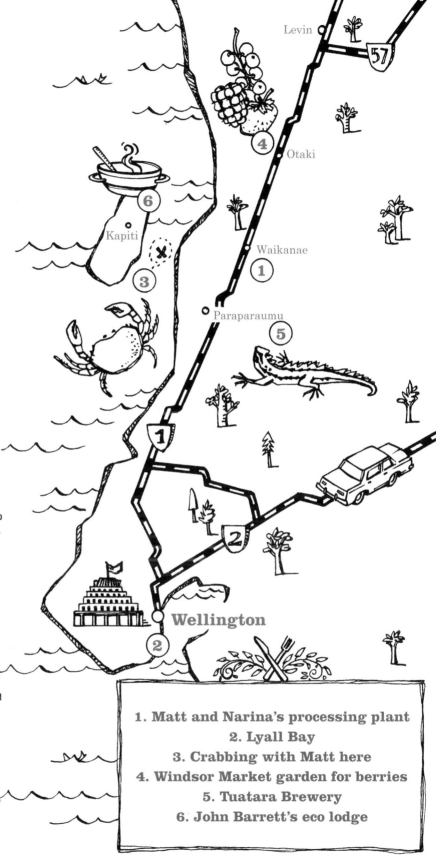

1. Matt and Narina's processing plant
2. Lyall Bay
3. Crabbing with Matt here
4. Windsor Market garden for berries
5. Tuatara Brewery
6. John Barrett's eco lodge

WAIKANAE CRAB CAKES WITH TARTARE SAUCE By Al Brown

I particularly love this style of dish for its simplicity and no-fuss presentation. A crab cake is a somewhat modest dish, but for many it's at the top of the comfort-food chain. There is a crunch on the outside, followed by moist, sweet, crab meat on the inside. Although it's relatively simple to prepare, there is an art to getting the mixture just right — using just enough mayo and breadcrumbs to hold the cakes together.

Serves 8 as an entrée.

STEP 1. TARTARE SAUCE

INGREDIENTS

1 cup Al's basic bach mayo mayonnaise (see page 19 or use ready made)

2 tablespoons capers, finely chopped

2 tablespoons red onion, finely chopped

¼ cup gherkins, finely chopped

2 tablespoons fresh parsley, finely chopped

½ tablespoon fresh tarragon, finely chopped

2 tablespoons wholegrain mustard

salt and pepper to taste

METHOD

Mix all the ingredients together until blended. Check the seasoning and add salt and pepper if required.

STEP 2. CRAB CAKES

INGREDIENTS

olive oil or canola oil for cooking

¼ cup celery, finely chopped

½ cup green capsicum, finely chopped

1 cup onion, finely chopped

½ tablespoon garlic, finely minced

500 g crab meat

¼ cup mayonnaise

1 teaspoon lemon juice

½ cup breadcrumbs

salt and pepper to season

extra breadcrumbs to coat cakes

lemon wedges to garnish

METHOD

Add a little oil to a small saucepan and, over low heat, sweat the celery, capsicum, onion and minced garlic. Cook for at least 30 minutes, stirring occasionally. Once the vegetables are soft and creamy, remove and cool to room temperature.

Put the vegetables, crab meat, mayonnaise and lemon juice in a bowl. Fold together then add the breadcrumbs to firm up the mixture. Season with salt and pepper and if the mixture seems too moist add some more breadcrumbs.

Mould the crab cakes to the size you require and lightly cover with breadcrumbs.

STEP 2. CRAB CAKES

Heat a little cooking oil in a medium-sized sauté pan over moderate heat. Cook the crab cakes on both sides until golden. Place in a preheated oven for 3 to 5 minutes, until warmed through. Serve on warm plates with a dollop of tartare sauce and a wedge of lemon.

CLEANING AND PREPARING CRABS

- Remove the 'back' of the crab, starting at the back and pulling forward towards the claws.

- Discard the back and remove any of the obvious guts.

- Now remove the 'feathers' that run along each side of the body.

- Remove the two main claws and also the end joints of the legs.

- Snap the body in half, exposing the crab meat.

- You now have the two main claws and two half bodies ready for cooking.

STEVE'S WINE RECOMMENDATION

Te Mata Woodthorpe Chardonnay from Hawke's Bay

Good Chardonnay always has a great structure without too many dominating flavours, so it tends to work well with food. This Hawke's Bay Chardonnay has nice ripe, rich, sweet fruit flavours that match the rich, sweet crab meat and creamy mayonnaise. The wine's citrus character helps to cleanse the palate between each mouthful, so each bite of crab is just as divine as the last. This wine was also served at Queen Elizabeth's eightieth birthday celebration.

MARLBOROUGH SCALLOPS

EXPLORING PRIME SCALLOP COUNTRY

For a long time, we've known how good the scallops from the Marlborough Sounds are and so were looking forward to scoring some fresh from the sea. We planned to toss them in a hot pan and serve them with a spicy corn and roasted capsicum salsa.

Our journey kicked off with a crossing on the Cook Strait ferry. There's always slight trepidation before a Cook Strait crossing — it can either be three gorgeous hours on flat blue ocean or the worst few hours of your life. This crossing had got off to a particularly stressful start when we had a rear-end fender-bender on the way to the ferry!

Sharing the crossing was the usual cross-section of humanity — foreign backpackers, school netball teams, biker clubs and frazzled parents trying to deal with out-of-control kids. It's all part of the ferry experience. We spent a bit of time leaning over the rails, revelling in what turned out to be a beautiful calm sailing. It wasn't long before we were cruising up Tory Channel — the entrance to the Marlborough Sounds, which is a network of ancient river-valley systems that were drowned as sea levels rose. There are all sorts of nooks and crannies among the multitude of waterways and islands.

Once off the ferry, we headed to East Bay, near the top of Arapawa Island in the Queen Charlotte Sound to meet brothers Nev and Trev Tahuaroa. They live in some prime scallop country and had invited us to stay and try some of their local shellfish.

GATEWAY TO THE SOUNDS

Picton's a cool little town. As the gateway to the South Island it has a lovely relaxed feel to it. The stress taken onto the ferry in Wellington was well out of the system by the time we rolled off in Picton.

For Steve it was a familiar sense of arrival. 'Our family bach is in the Sounds and I've been coming here the past 12 years. I love the isolation,

tranquillity and fishing, but I'd never been scalloping and it was time to change all that. To make sure I didn't miss out on any of the action, Al was going to get the wine,' said Steve.

Steve: On the ferry over we discussed at length the wine match for the scallops. Al was pretty keen on getting a Gewürztraminer, but I was sure a Pinot Gris would work best — I just had to hope Al could be relied on!

Before Al left on his mission to get the wine and ingredients for the salsa, he dropped Steve off at Beech Bay to meet Takutai and Pete Beech. They've been cruising the sounds in their classic launch, *Tutanekai,* for the last 10 years. Pete's family has lived in the Marlborough Sounds for six generations and were among the first Europeans to begin farming in the area. Takutai is of Ngaiterangi descent. She moved to the area years ago, met Pete and never left. That's not surprising given her name means 'one who has an affinity with the sea'. Both Takutai and Pete have a strong connection to the local environment and a sense of responsibility to protect it. They often take people out on *Tutanekai* to show them the wildlife along with explaining the Maori and European history of the region.

THE *TUTANEKAI* GOES TO EAST BAY

Steve: What I love about the Marlborough Sounds is that, regardless of the weather, the time of year or day, it always looks stunning. It's peaceful, quiet and very easy to feel as if you've got the place to yourself.

As Steve, Pete and Tak steamed their way slowly up Queen Charlotte Sound to East Bay, Al headed to Blenheim to get the wine and other ingredients for the scallop dish.

For Steve, the charm of being in the Sounds is that much of life there revolves around boats. Whether it's taking a ferry to get there, cruising the bays in a schooner, or being carted by water taxi, chances are if you are travelling in the area you're going to be travelling by boat. Boat-watching can be just as fascinating as people-watching and a lot can be said about a person's personality by the kind of boat they're in — there are gin palaces, old fishing boats, fizz boats, sail boats and kayaks, you name it.

Pete and Takutai's much-loved launch *Tutanekai* is a well-oiled vessel and it's in great nick. There's a classy canopy-covered seating area in the back where you can lounge about and take in the many bays and small settlements as they slide by.

Tutanekai was custom-built for the Sounds back in the 1930s — 42 foot and double masted, its flat-bottomed keel allows access to the many shallow beaches in the area. Not long into our journey, Pete turned the launch towards one of them. Approaching the shore, he lowered a stepladder over the bow and let Takutai and Steve off to search for some kaimoana while the tide was out. The native greenshell mussels are easy to gather off the rocks at low tide.

Steve and Takutai soon found a couple of good-sized mussels that would make a tasty snack as they steamed further up the Sounds. Greenshells are larger than other mussels and the flesh of male greenshell mussels is creamy in colour — the females are orange.

Back on deck, Takutai made paraoa or Maori bread to eat with the mussels. She combined self-raising flour, salt and water to make a dough that she divided into small scone-like shapes, which she fried quickly on both sides. 'The paraoa is kind of like a doughnut — it would be equally delicious with butter and a dollop of jam,' said Steve.

While the bread was frying, the mussels were steamed open and chopped into bite-sized pieces, ready to be sandwiched between the warm paraoa buns — it was an easy and delicious snack that anyone can make with only a few ingredients.

We continued up the Sounds and after about an hour's steaming, Pete deviated to Motuara Island, a predator-free bird sanctuary run by DOC. It's one of Pete's favourite places. About 50 metres out from the island Pete switched off the engine so they could hear the bird song — there was a wonderful mix of tui, bellbird and the rare saddleback — a real treat. Pete recalled the history of his ancestors:

'When my people first came to this area, they bought land off local Maori at Endeavour Inlet and they said it was just the most magnificent podocarp forest, with huge trees right to the water's edge. The thing that fascinated them more than anything was the birds, just thousands and thousands of them.'

But birds didn't provide the early settlers with income, farming did, and with it came the clearing of the bush. Pete continued his story:

'Our old people bought the land off the Maori in the mid-1800s. My great-grandfather spent his entire lifetime slashing and burning the bush. My grandfather pulled out stumps, but when it was time for my father to take over around the Second World War, the soil was bankrupt and scrub had started taking over.'

The clearing of land had a huge environmental impact on the Marlborough Sounds. Massive erosion saw large amounts of silt entering the sea. Burning of bush saw a loss of habitat for the native birds. To make things worse, the introduced weasels, stoats, rats, cats and other predators decimated the population of native birds. The tragedy is that that's what's happening throughout New Zealand today. The Department of Conservation has eradicated pests and the bush on this island is now coming on nicely — that's what makes this island so special.

It was at the top of Motuara Island, on 31 January 1770, that Captain Cook first formally raised the flag proclaiming British sovereignty over the South Island. This area of the Sounds is rich in the history of Captain Cook and because they were making such good time Pete and Tak steamed over to Ship Cove a few hundred metres across the water from Motuara Island.

In 1770, on his first voyage to New Zealand, Captain Cook anchored in Ship Cove. With a safe anchorage, running water, a good supply of food and plenty of timber to repair and maintain his ship, it became one of Cook's favoured hangouts on his three voyages to New Zealand, staying there five times between 1770 and 1777. Ship Cove is a gorgeous bay with a sandy beach and mature native trees coming down to the water. In fact, it looks relatively unchanged from the time that Cook visited, except for a monument to Cook and a beautifully carved pole depicting the great Maori explorer Kupe.

On the whole, Cook got along well with the local Maori and there would have been a fair amount of trading going on. Cook noted the lack of food sources for Maori and visiting sailors. So on subsequent voyages to New Zealand he brought a variety of plants and animals with him including the pig and the goat both of which are now well established in the area.

After the tour, it was time to get on with the main event — finding scallops. Steve, Takutai and Pete left Ship Cove to begin the last leg of their journey out to East Bay. It was a a good couple of hours away, which gave Steve plenty of time to wonder how Al had got on with getting the Pinot Gris.

SOURCING REGIONAL WINE AND PRODUCE

Al: I've always respected Steve's wine-matching skill — he's got a great palate and has taught me heaps. But having served my apprenticeship with him for 10 years, I have a growing amount of confidence in my own selections.

Driving through Marlborough's vast Wairau Valley with miles and miles of well-kept, well-ordered and well-watered vineyards, Al couldn't help but be impressed — on one side are parched rolling hills, on the other a high mountain range and in between a massive, rich-green canopy of vines.

Marlborough is one of the most famous wine regions in the Southern Hemisphere, known especially for its Sauvignon Blanc. The first of the new-era plantings began in 1973 and the planting hasn't stopped. Vineyards have pushed out into the traditional farming country.

One of these vineyards is Seresin Estate, which Al and Steve have had a strong relationship with since Logan Brown. Al knew their wine would be great, but the question remained, what would go best with the scallops?

Al turned off the main Wairau Valley Road at the large rock with Seresin's distinctive hand logo and an arrow. He followed his nose down a gravel road to the vineyard where he met Seresin's viticulturist, a very knowledgeable and likeable Aussie. Colin Ross exudes passion for all things organic and biodynamic, which is what Seresin is known for.

Colin explained the meaning of biodynamic to Al. Literally translated, bio means life and dynamic to move. 'What biodynamic growers endeavour to do is to enrich and enhance the life of their soil. The thing we're most proud of is our soil,' said Colin.

Fundamental to biodynamics is creating a concentrated form of compost. This is done in purpose-built underground pits where Colin combines a range of organic matter, including cow manure, egg shells and various herbal concoctions. The concentrated mixture is put into a barrel of water and stirred for a good hour to 'activate' it before spreading over the vineyard.

After a quick tour of the vineyard it was time to pick the wine that would best go with our planned dish of pan-seared scallops with corn and pepper

thymebank

steve and takutai

steve, trev and al

pete and nev

check 'em out

trev and takutai

salsa. Colin uncorked a Gewürztraminer and a Pinot Gris on the bonnet of the Holden. After much tasting and discussion of both wines, it seemed the Gewürz would work a treat, but the Pinot Gris was magnificent, too. Not wanting to cross Mr Logan, Al took a couple of bottles of each. And for good measure he nabbed a bottle of their outstanding lemon-infused olive oil which would be a natural fit for the scallops.

With the extra bottles added to the cellar in the boot of the Holden, all Al had to get now was the ingredients for the salsa.

THYMEBANK

For years, Thymebank herbs have been used at Logan Brown so Al was keen to take the opportunity to visit the herb farm and meet the owner Martyn Birch. After grabbing some fresh coriander Martyn showed Al a range of chillies growing in his tunnel house, explaining the rule of thumb — the smaller the chillies, the more intense the heat and flavour.

HITCHING A RIDE UP THE SOUNDS

With fresh herbs on board, Al collected fresh sweetcorn and capsicums from a roadside stall on his way back to Picton. He was heading to the mail-boat depot, to get a ride to East Bay. 'At this point, I was beginning to get a little envious of Steve's half-day head start. I didn't like the idea of him getting to those scallops before me,' said Al. It was time to get cracking.

The mail boats are a great way to get around the Sounds and Al reckoned that if he got the timing right he had a good chance of arriving at East Bay before Steve. Unfortunately, he didn't get it right. In fact, he couldn't have got it more wrong and missed the boat by 10 minutes — and the next one wasn't leaving for two days! 'Try the marina' was the best offer he got.

There's always plenty of action at Picton Marina, with boaties picking up supplies, dropping off guests and loading ice. Al wandered around, desperately looking for a familiar face and it wasn't too long before he spotted someone he had seen in the restaurant, Andrew Meehan. Unfortunately, Andrew wasn't heading to East Bay, but he was passing close by. So with the promise of a night out at Logan Brown, Al was soon speeding up the Sounds towards East Bay.

ARRIVING AT EAST BAY

The sun was sitting low in the sky by the time *Tutanekai* steamed into East Bay on Arapawa Island. It is a large bay, roughly a kilometre across, surrounded by steep hills, covered in a mix of scrub, bush and pasture. In the corner of the bay is a wharf and waiting for them there with a welcoming grin from ear to ear was one of life's great characters — Nev Tahuaroa.

Al: All salsas generally have fresh herbs of some sort in them and for a summer salsa, I never go past fresh coriander as one of the components. It has such a unique flavour unlike any other herb. Coriander lends itself particularly well to spicy food, adding a flavour and fragrance that holds its own against the other competing ingredients such as chillies, lime juice and spices.

SCALLOPS

Fan-shaped scallops are found all around New Zealand, particularly in bays with waters 10–50 m deep. The ribbed upper shell is flat and the ribbed lower shell is curved.

Scallops have a tiny row of eyes just below the upper shell.

Unlike other bivalve shellfish, scallops can swim. Mostly, they lie on the sea floor and filter feed. When danger threatens they contract a powerful muscle that shoots out water, propelling them to safety.

Two types of scallops are commercially fished in New Zealand: the large *Pecten novazelandiae* from the top of the South Island; and *Zygochlamys delicatula*, the brightly coloured queen scallop from the deep waters off the Otago coast.

The legal catch size limit for scallops is 100 mm in most parts of the country, but it's 90 mm in the Marlborough Sounds and Challenger fishery management area.

In most areas of New Zealand recreational fishers may fish for scallops from 15 July to 14 February.

Scallops may spawn several times annually, normally between September and April. Most scallops are sexually mature at around 60 mm, releasing millions of eggs before reaching the minimum catch size.

Pete, Tak and Steve loaded their gear into an amazing looking six-wheeled contraption that Nev had bought on TradeMe. It looked a bit like a moon buggy but was ideal for getting everything around the couple of hundred metres of rocky foreshore to Nev's house, where Steve met Nev's wife, Gaye.

While Steve was being looked after by Nev, his brother Trev headed away in the boat to pick up Al who had been dropped off at their neighbours' place. Trev lives in Australia most of the year but returns to the family land at Onauku in East Bay every year.

Nev and Trev are Te Atiawa, originally from northern Taranaki, and are direct descendants of one of the paramount chiefs. Their ancestors came to this area in the mid-1820s, took possession of the land, and have occupied it ever since. They are regarded as the tangata whenua of Onauku, Arapawa Island.

In the hallway of the homestead Nev showed Steve a piece of the original waka, *Paora*, that their great-great-grandfather left Taranaki and crossed Cook Strait in. When 20 waka left Porirua Harbour, they hit some very bad storms and 10 waka went down. Many lives were lost. The brothers had an amazing knowledge of their history and both felt strongly that a member of the whanau should always be present on the land, which is why Nev and Gaye moved back there from Auckland two years ago.

That evening we all sat around the kitchen table in the homestead and shared plenty of laughs, some fascinating history, cold beer and Gaye's delicious, home-baked savouries. And to top it off, the tide wasn't in until 10 the next morning so we could have a bit of a lie-in in preparation for the long-awaited opportunity to snorkel for scallops.

SNORKELLING FOR SCALLOPS

The next day was one out of the box with a cloudless sky, warm weather and clear water. Al, Steve and Trev made their way around the bay to a scalloping spot Trev had lined up and got into wetsuits. Al and Steve were scalloping on the snorkel which is a big ask, even in the plentiful waters of East Bay. To make sure they got enough for a feed, Trev was sent out on the tanks. As they all entered the water, he was full of useful advice. 'You're heading in the right direction . . . anywhere out to sea will do!'

New Zealand scallops are found in sandy-bottomed bays all around the country, usually in waters from 10–50 m deep. In less fished areas, such as East Bay, you can find them in shallower waters. We searched for signs of the scallop's distinctive ribbed shell but, despite the great visibility, they weren't that easy to find.

You can either dive for scallops or dredge for them, but dragging a dredge turns over everything in its path damaging the sea floor. It seemed far better to hand select the shellfish from the sea floor rather than ruin the delicate environment that they grow in.

After an hour or so of solid searching Al and Steve managed to pick up half

Al: I simply love cooking in bach kitchens. With a wood-burning stove, small gas grill, dinky little sink and limited equipment, it is a challenge to knock out a great dish. But it's always great fun, too.

a dozen between them. That was nowhere near enough to feed everyone so it was up to Trev — and he didn't disappoint. Al and Steve were comparing their meagre catch when he finally emerged like Santa Claus, his dive bag bulging with large, succulent East Bay scallops.

Al opened one and ate it straight from the shell. It was everything he'd expected — fat, firm, juicy and absolutely gorgeous. The next thing to do was to head back to Trev's and shuck the catch.

Trev had the perfect scallop-shucking set-up — an old table on the deck, the high tide lapping at his feet and, out in front, a magnificent view over the bay. With a glass of wine in hand, Trev effortlessly shucked his scallops, using a knife to open the shell and remove the scallop, leaving the guts behind. 'It was a typical Kiwi scene — Trev sitting on the deck of his bach filled with memories, having exerted a good amount of effort to gather the ingredients before him,' said Steve.

THE COOK-UP

Scallops are a favourite seafood of many New Zealanders, for their sweetness and texture. We've eaten scallops from many different locations in New Zealand. All are wonderful, but the Nelson scallop is, for us, unparalleled. It's slightly smaller than other scallops, but has a subtly more silken, yet firm texture that carmelises beautifully and never leeches liquid. We can eat them raw by the dozen, unadorned or with a squeeze of lemon juice.

With a great sense of satisfaction we sat and surveyed the beautiful bay before us. Only hours before, we had harvested the magnificent scallops on the table and we were reminded of how fortunate we are to live in New Zealand. We toasted our good fortune and our new mates Nev and Trev!

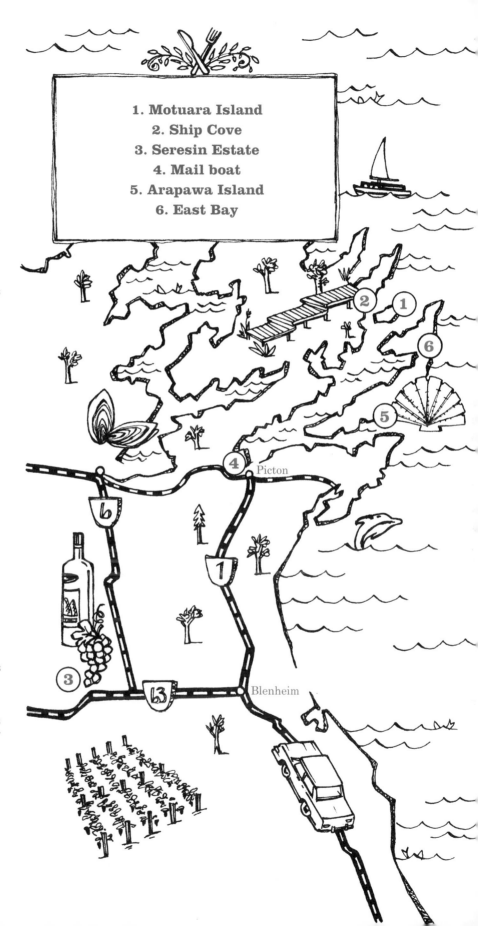

A SHORT HISTORY OF THIS REGION

The population is around 40,000, with the largest proportion — 26,000 — living in Blenheim.

The first Polynesian settlers arrived around AD1000.

Abel Tasman spent a week in Cook Strait in 1642, but James Cook was the first European to visit the Marlborough Sounds and the place he named Ship Cove in 1770. He made two further visits to the Marlborough Sounds in 1774 and 1777.

In 1826, Captain John Guard established the first land-based whaling station at Cloudy Bay and the sealers and whalers arrived.

In 1829, Colonel Edward Gibbon Wakefield of the New Zealand Company arrived at Ship Cove to begin a survey with a view to establishing a colony in the area.

On 17 June 1840, British sovereignty was proclaimed over the South Island on Horahora Kakahu Island, by Major Bunbury.

In 1973, Montana began the first commercial vineyard plantings in the area. Marlborough is now one of the most important wine-growing regions in the southern hemisphere. It has gained worldwide recognition for its excellent Sauvignon Blanc production.

Some pastoral farming continues, but this is much reduced due to the high prices that are being paid for land suitable for viticulture. Tourism centred around the wine industry is growing, but the region is also known for its natural beauty, outdoor activities and eco tourism. Greenshell mussel farming in the Sounds is one of Marlborough's largest industries.

1. Motuara Island
2. Ship Cove
3. Seresin Estate
4. Mail boat
5. Arapawa Island
6. East Bay

Picton

Blenheim

SEARED SCALLOPS WITH FRESH CORN AND RED CAPSICUM SALSA By Al Brown

Scallops and corn have always gone together. Add some roasted capsicum, spices such as toasted cumin and smoked paprika, lime juice and coriander, a little lemon-infused olive oil to mix it together and it just works. It's fresh and light, a perfect summertime lunch dish, with distinctive sharp fresh flavours.

Before cooking the scallops, dry them off, so that they caramelise nicely without stewing. Be careful not to use too much chilli to avoid overpowering the delicate shellfish. We want spice as well as heat, so the dry-roasted cumin seeds give the dish some added life.

Serves 8–10 as an appetiser.

STEP 1. FRESH CORN AND RED CAPSICUM SALSA

INGREDIENTS
3 cups cooked corn kernels
1 cup roasted red peppers, seeds and stalks removed, finely diced
¼ cup red onion, finely diced
¼ cup fresh coriander, finely chopped
½–1 fresh chilli, finely diced
1 tablespoon ground cumin seeds
½ tablespoon smoked sweet paprika
½ tablespoon sugar
2 tablespoons lemon juice, extra to taste
½ cup lemon oil
salt and freshly ground black pepper to taste

METHOD
In a bowl break up the corn kernels. Add all the other ingredients and stir together. Season to taste with extra lemon juice, salt and black pepper.

Store in the fridge until required.

STEP 2. SERVING

INGREDIENTS
oil
50–60 fresh scallops patted dry with paper towel
fresh corn and red capsicum salsa
lemons or limes to garnish

METHOD
Heat a grill or griddle plate to very hot. Oil and season the scallops and divide
into two batches. Divide the corn salsa evenly onto individual serving plates.
Take the first batch of scallops and place on the grill. Cook for no longer than
45 seconds on each side. Remove and place on the salsa, repeat with second
batch. Garnish with a wedge of lime or lemon and serve pronto!

STEVE'S WINE RECOMMENDATION

Seresin Marlborough Pinot Gris

Seresin produces really full-flavoured concentrated wines, so their Pinot
Gris has enough grunt to stand up to the robust corn salsa but, also, enough
finesse to allow the flavour of the scallops to shine through. Like a squeeze
of lemon juice, the wine's acidity adds a nice zing to the combination.

The Gewürz that Al also brought with him was a nice match for the
scallops on their own, but the roasted corn in the salsa dominated the lovely
characteristics of the wine.

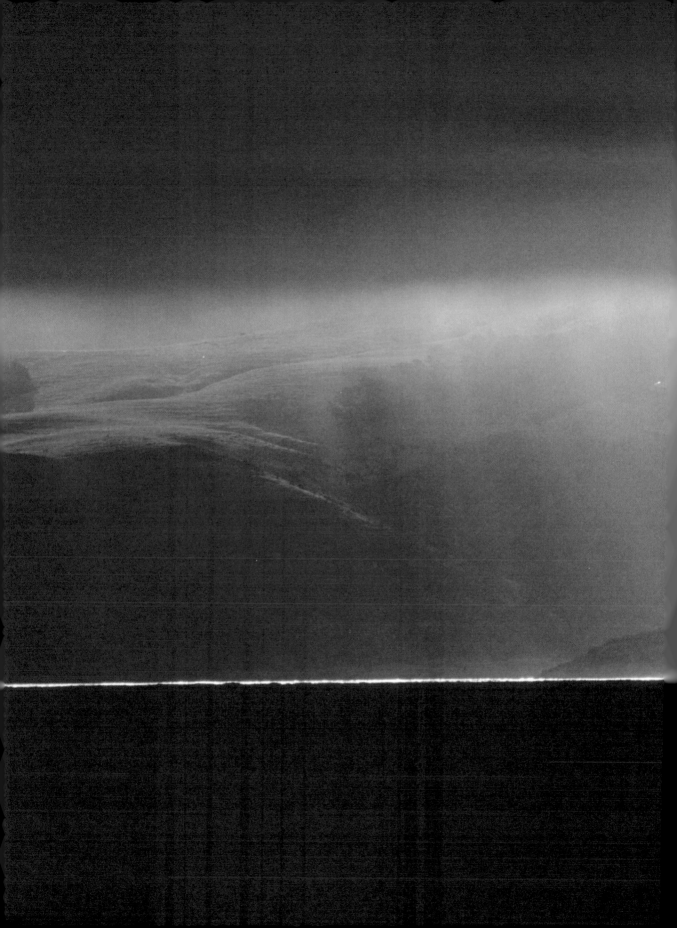

EELS ON
BANKS PENINSULA

THE MYSTERIOUS EEL

Most of us think of the eel as the slimy, dark and mysterious creature we spent many childhood hours chasing up streams and in swamps. We knew very little about them and our trip to Banks Peninsula was full of promise and possibility.

As we journeyed down the southern side of the peninsula we were about to learn a lot about this intriguing New Zealand native that is found in swamps and waterways all over the country.

We planned to hook up with a local kaumatua for a traditional eel harvest, meet a scientist who has studied eels for over 30 years and help a commercial eeler with his catch. To finish, we were planning to prepare a dish of smoked eel with a horseradish and cauliflower purée.

Before heading out to find eels in the wild, we decided to take a close look at some pets at Willowbank Wildlife Reserve in Christchurch — the eels took a shine to the jellymeat on offer and slid out of the water and up the steps to devour it. Up close, it was easy to see why people are put off by these slimy creatures.

'Just looking at eels is enough to put me off my appetite. Normally I buy smoked eel in nice little packets and it's all golden and boneless. I started off thinking eeling wouldn't be the most scintillating hunting-and-gathering experience I'd ever have, but I was happy to be proved wrong,' said Steve.

HEADING TO BANKS PENINSULA

From Christchurch, the road to Banks Peninsula runs round the base of the Port Hills, crossing fertile flats before it reaches the rolling foothills of the peninsula. As it nears the coast, it skirts around Lake Ellesmere or Te Waihora, New Zealand's fourth-largest lake. Tucked in beside Lake Ellesmere there is the smaller Lake Forsyth or Wairewa. These lakes are renowned for their eels and, for centuries, have provided local Maori with this highly valued food source.

After a 45-minute drive we arrived at Birdlings Flat, a small holiday settlement on Kaitorete Spit at the southern end of Lake Forsyth. Kaitorete Spit is a huge shingle barrier extending south for 20-odd kilometres separating lakes Ellesmere and Forsyth from the open sea. It's a wild, rugged and exposed piece of coastline.

Local kaumatua and eeling legend George Skipper lives at Birdlings Flat. George was born in the area almost 80 years ago and his runanga has exclusive eeling rights for Wairewa. We were lucky enough to be joining him to learn the traditional way of catching, smoking and preserving eel.

PRESERVING THE EEL WITH GEORGE

Al: I'd never been to this part of the country before. Driving around, I could see it had a real rawness about it — it was unforgiving, cold, windswept and slightly hostile. It's not where I'd normally want to go for a holiday, but it has its own sort of beauty.

George's place was in prime position — he had the closest house to the sea and it was also on the lakefront, a stone's throw from where Al and Steve were going to be catching eels. When they arrived George was busy processing the eels he'd caught the night before.

George obviously came from an era where people didn't throw anything away — there was stuff everywhere, scattered in strategic places around his section — there were spare parts from cars, chairs on their last recline, old freezers and a number of other things that just might come in handy one day.

George showed Al and Steve a sack of eels that he'd had sitting in salt overnight. He grabbed one and stripped the sticky, snot-like slime off it. The sight of that was enough to send Al running and, with Al gone, Steve and George got to work.

During the season, which runs from late summer through to autumn, George goes eeling whenever the conditions allow. Eels are considered a delicacy to his people and he's kept busy most of the season catching and preserving eel for hui and other gatherings up and down the country. It's done in the time-honoured, traditional way.

After taking the slime off the rest of the eels in the sack, Steve helped George hang them by their heads on wooden racks. With a pair of old hand-shears George snipped the tail to let them bleed. This begins the preservation process and helps to set the flesh.

When the flesh is firm enough, the next step is to remove the backbone. George moved the eel to a table and cut the head off. Then, he carefully cuts along each side of the backbone and as he removed it, two large fillets of eel were opened up exposing the flesh for drying. These were then hung on an old wooden A-frame rack and left overnight to dry in the Canterbury wind to be smoked the next day.

George had obviously been taught not to waste any of this precious resource because there was barely any flesh on the back bone left for the gathering seagulls. Those that waited were rewarded with the guts and creamy fat, which they demolished greedily.

Local Maori have been preserving eels like this for centuries and the lake area has long been known as the food basket of the region. It was a wonderful resource and the ability to provide an all-year-round supply of preserved food brought a lot of mana to the local people. 'The food was great for bartering. People would come and visit and they would bring mussels, paua or crayfish. Muttonbirds were a big trader too — that was the system,' said George.

THE MYSTERIOUS EEL MIGRATION

Every autumn, thousands of eels all over New Zealand start a remarkable and mysterious journey. It begins with a desire to mate and an urge to move to the open sea and ends some 4000 kilometres later somewhere in the South Pacific. It's a one-way trip to mate before they die. Al was looking forward to finding out a bit more about the eel and its mysterious migration.

Al was headed for the southern side of Lake Ellesmere, where he had arranged to meet NIWA scientist Don Jellyman, who has been studying the eel for over 30 years. When Al arrived, Don was knee-deep in water next to a foldaway table with a measuring cradle on it. Beside him was a bucket full of anaesthetised eels.

Don was monitoring the weight and length of migrating eels and Al lent him a helping hand. Don's past studies have included putting tracking tags on large longfin eels to try to find out where they go. When the tags dislodge they send data back via satellite. From that information, Don has found that eels will swim to depths of up to one kilometre during the day and rise to depths of 100–200 metres at night. They will take three to four months to reach their spawning grounds, but the million-dollar question remains unanswered: Where do the eels go? While no one knows for sure, it is generally believed they head off to spawning grounds in the area of Vanuatu, Samoa or Fiji.

Once eels enter the sea they don't eat, so before migration they fatten up to build reserves for the long journey. The egg-bearing females — a good-sized female will probably have 20 million eggs — are three to four times larger than the males. In a remarkable feat of nature, the males know to leave many weeks before the faster-swimming females, so that they all arrive at the spawning grounds at the same time. Whether male or female, the urge to mate is coupled with a strong urge to get out of the lake and this is triggered by a variety of conditions.

'With a high tide at night and a southerly blowing, waves crash over the spit and a bit of salt water washes over — the eels get really cranked up and are up and wriggling over the spit to reach the saltwater,' said Don.

DIGGING THE EELING DRAINS

George and his people have known about the migrating eels for centuries and at Wairewa they have developed a unique way of catching them.

Al: For us, eels have always been shrouded with a certain amount of mystery and folklore. Growing up, we heard stories about them moving across land in storms when it's wet, but we never knew why.

The lake is land-locked for most of the year — the gravel of Kaitorete Spit creates a barrier between the lake and the sea. By digging drains into the gravel spit at the end of the lake, they cleverly trap the migrating eels as they try to reach the ocean.

At the start of each season, the drains are dug about one metre across by 20 metres long with a small pool at the end of each. They have to be deep enough to trick the eels into thinking they're the shortest way out of the lake.

During the season, before each night's eeling, the drains usually require a bit of attention. With the last lot of eels all processed and hanging to dry, Steve and George got on the end of a shovel each and started work, digging out gravel to widen each drain to allow the water to flow. It was back-breaking work, but great exercise and after an hour on the end of the shovel the drains were complete. All there was to do now was to wait for night and hope for the right conditions — good cloud cover and a decent wind to push water into the drains. With a bit of down time Steve took the opportunity to check out George's throne — an old La-Z-Boy chair sitting on a pallet in front of his house with a footstool appropriately placed in front. Like everything else at George's, it looked as if it was just put there without any thought, but once he'd nestled in Steve could see it was in the perfect position. 'It's pretty rough and basic, but it's ideal. From there, George could survey the hills, the sea, and his eel drains. He's got all he needs and he's got his family near him. I can see why he's such a peaceful man,' said Steve.

COMMERCIAL EELING ON LAKE ELLESMERE

While Steve and George were doing the hard yards, Al was continuing his research. Next on his list was a visit to Clem Smith who has been commercially eeling on Lake Ellesmere for the past 30 years. Al caught up with Clem at the boat ramp as he was about to go and clear his nets that had been soaking overnight and jumped onboard to join him.

At 23 kilometres wide and 13 kilometres long, Lake Ellesmere is New Zealand's fourth-largest lake, but it was once a lot larger than it is today. It used to be part of a huge wetland that extended towards Christchurch and well into the Canterbury plains. European settlers drained large areas of the shallow lake and turned the reclaimed land into pasture. At the time Ngai Tahu protested strongly about the loss of their traditional fishery, but draining of the swamp continued, further shrinking the lake.

The eels that live in the lake are fished commercially by Clem and four other eel fishers who work a few months every year until their quota is filled. There are two sorts of eels in New Zealand — longfin and shortfin. On the day that Al went out with Clem, he was targeting eels that could be frozen and sent to London to be turned into jellied eel, a Cockney favourite. Al couldn't believe his eyes when he first saw the mass of squirming eels in Clem's net. They were emptied into a sorting bin and Clem showed Al how to distinguish the males from the females, the longfin from the shortfin. All except the shortfinned males were released back into the lake that day.

All the eels were starting to make Al feel a bit peckish, but not being one for jellied eel, he headed to Aquahaven Seafoods on the banks of Lake Ellesmere, where much of the eel from the lake is processed and smoked for the local market.

Al: The first thing that struck me was how beautiful they are — they're all slightly different shades of gold, silver, brown and tan and their eyes are incredibly sharp and beautiful. There was something very tactile about putting your hands into a mass of slimy, squirming eel.

al and the two mandys

al with don
jellyman

george's eel drying

blending horseradish

al clem and an 80 year
old female

al steve and george at lake
forsyth

SMOKED EEL PATÉ

Smoked is Al's favourite way to eat eel and the visit to Aquahaven was a great opportunity to see how smoking is done on a commercial scale. While there he also picked up enough to make a smoked eel pâté to share with Steve before they went out for the night to catch more eel. It's a simple thing to make and Al whipped it up on the boot of the Holden.

INGREDIENTS

smoked eel
sour cream
small amount of runny cream
fresh herbs such as chives, dill, basil, tarragon
lemon juice
salt and pepper to taste

METHOD

Chop up the eel as coarsely or as fine as you desire. Add some sour cream and a little runny cream and mix together to a spreadable consistency. Add some chopped herbs, a squeeze of lemon juice and season with salt and pepper.

This simple recipe also works well with smoked salmon and most other smoked fish.

Al: The beauty of smoked eel is that it's so versatile —it goes just as well in a sandwich, dressed up to serve as an hors d'oeuvre, in a Japanese dish, or as part of an antipasto platter.

MANDYS HORSERADISH SAUCE

Before meeting back up with Steve and George, Al had one key ingredient to get for his eel dish — horseradish. In Canterbury there are not many people that know more about horseradish than the two Mandys. Mandy Kain and Mandy Steel grow and harvest horseradish all year round, and transform it into their famous horseradish sauce, which Al has been a fan of for years. 'Mandys Horseradish Sauce has a nice amount of sweetness, but the kick of a crazy horse. I go through jars of it at home, serving it with anything and everything. I just love that hot bite that marries so well with all the other flavours,' said Al.

Horseradish is a perennial plant of the brassica family. It grows up to 1.5 metres tall and is cultivated mainly for its large, white, tapering root.

When Al drove up, the Mandys were using an old tractor-drawn potato harvester to lift the roots out of the ground. 'We actually find that at this time of year when the leaves are going into their dormant phase that the radish is at its hottest,' said Mandy Steel.

After harvesting and cleaning the horseradish, comes the peeling and chopping. Like onions there is no aroma until the horseradish is cut, but once it is, the plants produce an incredibly strong mustard oil, which stings your throat and eyes. Al learnt that lesson the hard way!

Given the option of wearing goggles, Al foolishly turned Mandy down. Horseradish throws out 100 times the choking power of a chopped onion. When they blended the radish Al took a good sniff and ended up coughing and

Al: When I was a kid I used to love catching frogs and eels. After school, the boy next door and I would jump on bikes and take off to the Whangaehu River looking for eels. Armed with a piece of wood with twine round it, a good-sized fish hook and some hunks of dog tucker for bait we were all set. We used to catch eels for fun, but when the shearing gangs were at the farm, we would swap them with the Maori shearers for fizzy drinks or chocolate bars. Very early on, Maori had recognised the good eating qualities of eels. I eventually cottoned on too. Now, as a chef, I've come to love New Zealand smoked eel.

choking for ages — it was totally debilitating. 'I then went for the swimming goggles and by the end of it, had the full gas mask,' says Al.

Once the horseradish has been finely blended, the final step is adding it to the Mandys' top-secret base sauce. With a jar to take away, all that Al needed now was some eel.

NIGHT EELING WITH GEORGE

By the time Al got back to Birdlings Flat the sun was almost down and he was greeted by an excited Steve. The wind had picked up and was pushing water into the drains that he and George had worked on earlier in the day. The moon was coming and going through broken cloud — ideally there would be no moon, as the eels run better on a moonless night.

Al and Steve shared the smoked eel paté and a beer while they waited for night to fall and for George to join them. They were both looking forward to seeing first-hand the traditional way of eel fishing. Eventually, George wandered up. He had an old torch and three fibreglass poles, each with a sharp barbless hook on the end. These were to be used for gaffing the eels out of the drains. In the old days they would have been made out of manuka, but otherwise very little has changed over the years.

Rugged up against the cold and with gaffs and headlamps ready to go, Al, Steve and George sat quietly on the edge of the lake for a good half hour to give the migrating eels time to make their way up the drain. When George gave the word, they silently made their way to the entrance of the drain.

George whispered instructions: 'Work your way up the drain.' When Al and Steve got the nod they turned their lights on and were into it, both of them ripping the gaff blindly through the water hoping to snare an eel. The plan was to push the eels ahead of them and into the small pool at the end of each drain. The water was deep at the drain's entrance but as they got further up it became shallower.

They watched George whip an eel out. It looked simple enough but, as Al and Steve found out, there was quite a knack to getting a slippery eel out of a drain and onto the bank.

It took a good few attempts and a certain amount of laughter and hoping, but eventually both Al and Steve managed to hook onto an eel. The eels had plenty of fight and they had to be gaffed in one quick movement. It was a real rush and not too dissimilar to their childhood memories of catching eels.

At the end of the drains, the three of them retired to the bank for 30 minutes to allow a new wave of migrating eels to enter the drains. Then they started all over again.

They did this several times throughout the night and each time there were more eels in the drains. It was great fun — a heady mix of adrenalin and testosterone that comes with any sort of hunt or chase.

By the end of the night they had a sackful of eels. It had been a great night out and it was easy to see why George was still at it after 70-odd years.

EELS

New Zealand has two native freshwater eels, easily distinguished by the length of their dorsal fins. The longfin eel (*Anguilla dieffenbachii*) lives mainly in high country lakes and stony rivers. The shortfin eel (*Anguilla australis*) is found more abundantly and closer to the coast in lagoons, coastal lakes such as Waihora, and muddy rivers. In 1996, a third species from Australia was found in the North Island, the Australian longfin (*Anguilla reinhardtii*).

The life span of eels is 20–40 years, but a few have been known to live much longer.

Migrating eels leave around March and April each year to breed. They travel long distances and are thought to spawn somewhere around Fiji, Samoa or Vanuatu before they die.

After spawning, the tiny elvers drift back on ocean currents, eventually reaching the river systems in New Zealand.

Due to wetland drainage and pollution, there are fewer habitats for eels in New Zealand now and some river obstructions have prevented their migration. Elvers are regularly transferred to hydro lakes, farm dams, or headwaters that are land locked to provide additional stock for these areas.

Eels were first harvested for export in the late 1960s, and are sold in Europe and Japan.

Recreational fishers can legally take six eels a day, regardless of size.

Commercially there is a national minimum size of 220 g and in the South Island there is also a maximum legal size of 4 kg to provide some protection for the older female longfin eels.

Freshwater eels or tuna are prized in Maori culture, particularly for hui and tangi. They were a particularly important food source south of the Banks Peninsula where the staple kumara did not grow. Maori traditionally used a range of methods to gather eels, including eel pots or hinaki, eel weirs, nets, spears and trenches.

In 1868, several Maori fishing reserves were established in Canterbury by the government to honour a promise made to Ngai Tahu when it was purchased in the Kemp Deed.

There are also a number of lakes and rivers designated as non-commercial eel fisheries, but also some waterways like Lake Forsyth and its tributaries where the eels are the exclusive right of Ngai Tahu under Maori customary rights.

SMOKING EEL GEORGE'S WAY

The next day dawned crisp and clear. The eel George and Steve had hung the day before had dried well overnight, developing a crusty skin. Steve cut slits in the flesh to get it ready for smoking and noticed the large amount of oil coming through the surface of the flesh.

George had a large rudimentary smoker, designed to take a lot of eels at once. Steve rubbed salt and brown sugar into the eel before hanging it on the rack. George lit a small fire, and added the 'cough medicine' — he used manuka sawdust to give a good smoky flavour. The door was closed and the cabinet was covered with sacks to keep the smoke in. It took about four hours for the eel to cook and get a good flavour, so Steve left George and went to find a nice bottle of local wine to go with the dish Al was about to rustle up.

SOURCING LOCAL WINE

Grant: Pinot noir should be about texture. It is a feminine wine — the sort of wine to savour with a close friend, when more than two is a crowd.

Given that in Maori, kai means food and tuna means eel, it was fitting that our wine for this dish came from Kaituna Valley Wines on Banks Peninsula.

On the day Steve visited Grant Whelan, the winemaker, he had a mobile plant in for the day bottling Steve's favourite wine — Pinot Noir. Grant uses a contract bottling plant and it works extremely well for the small winery. 'They pull in, we feed in bottles at one end, add the wine and carton-up at the other end,' Grant said.

The Pinot at Kaituna comes from 30-year-old plants, tucked in on the side of a north-facing hill. 'I think our wines probably tend to have a bit more complexity about them. They're not like Central Otago fruit bombs. They tend to be a little more complex, a little more structured,' said Grant.

Despite Grant's recommendations, there would be three sharing this Pinot, so with a couple of bottles in hand, Steve returned to Birdlings Flat to pick up George and check on the eel. When it came out of the smoker it looked absolutely beautiful. Steve and George headed off to find Al who was preparing the dish in a bach on the edge of Wairewa and even he was impressed.

DINNER WITH GEORGE

It had been an amazing couple of days and sharing the rewards was a fitting finale. George has a ton of mana — he's softly spoken, very gentle, with a great sense of humour and a fantastic laugh. He's as sharp as a tack and could recall All Black games and players from the 1940s and 1950s as if it was yesterday. That was a real blast for us.

Of all the hunting and gathering adventures we'd had, this was the most surprising of all — we now have a huge respect for the mystical eel and its undiscovered secrets.

A SHORT HISTORY OF THIS REGION

Banks Peninsula is near Christchurch, in Canterbury. The population is around 8000, with 96 per cent of European origin.

There were three successive phases of Maori settlement in the area, which was called Horomaka. First, it was settled by Waitaha, followed by Kati Mamoe and, finally, in the seventeenth century by Ngai Tahu.

Sometimes the area is called Te Pataka o Rakaihautu — the food storehouse of the Paramount Chief Rakaihautu — recognising the rich resources the area has to offer, including whitebait, eels and kokopu from freshwater lakes and streams, berries and birds from the land, and shellfish, fish and crayfish from the coastal areas.

Captain Cook on the *Endeavour* first sighted the peninsula on 16 February 1770 and mistakenly concluded that it was an island. He named it after Joseph Banks, the ship's botanist. Later in 1809, when Captain S Chase tried to sail around it in the vessel *Pegasus*, he discovered that it was a peninsula.

In the early nineteenth century sealers and whalers came to the area. During the 1830s the whalers traded flax and food with Maori.

The French planned a settlement at Akaroa in 1839, but when the first settlers arrived in 1840, they found that the British had already claimed sovereignty over the whole country.

British settlers formed small settlements around Akaroa and Lyttelton harbours. Before settlement, much of the land was covered in podocarp forest. Clearing the forest for farmland meant sawmilling provided much employment for the early settlers — estimates suggest that about 75 per cent of the forest had been felled by 1870.

A 2.5 km-long railway tunnel linking Christchurch and Lyttelton was opened in 1867. A two-lane road tunnel opened alongside the railway tunnel in 1964.

Cheese was one of the first products exported from the region in the mid-nineteenth century and commercial cheese-making was well established by the 1890s.

The 20,000-hectare Lake Ellesmere is the largest lake in the Canterbury region. Since Europeans settled the area and drained large parts of the shallow lake for farmland, it is about half its original size.

In 1988, ownership of the lake bed was returned to the Ngai Tahu people, who hold customary fishing rights to the area.

1. Lake Ellesmere
2. Lake Forsyth
3. Birdlings flat
4. Kaitorete spit
5. Don Jellyman looks at eels
6. Aquahaven seafoods
7. Two Mandys horseradish
8. Kaituna Vineyard

73

Christchurch

1

75

Selwyn Huts

Leeston

Southbridge

8

6

5

1

2

3

4

SMOKED EEL WITH HORSERADISH CAULIFLOWER PURÉE, CRISP CURRANTS AND PINE NUTS By Al Brown

This to me is a terrific dish, as all its components work together — it just makes sense. The richness of the smoked eel is cut by the acid and sharpness of the horseradish. The cauliflower acts as a foil and adds a slightly savoury flavour, while the pine nuts and oven-roasted currants have all the textures covered — it 'eats' beautifully!

Serves 8 as an entrée.

STEP 1. HORSERADISH CAULIFLOWER PURÉE

INGREDIENTS
1 cauliflower, cut into bite-sized pieces
1½ cups cream
130 g Mandys Horseradish Sauce (½ a jar)
lemon juice to taste
salt and white pepper to taste

METHOD
Place a saucepan of salted water on the heat and bring to the boil. Add the cauliflower and cook for 7–10 minutes, until slightly soft.

Remove from the heat and strain off the water. Add the cream and horseradish to the cauliflower and place the saucepan back on the heat. Cook for another 5 minutes until the liquid is slightly reduced.

Pour the cauliflower mixture into a liquidiser and purée until smooth. Strain through a fine sieve discarding any of the tough pieces of horseradish. Add a squeeze of lemon juice and salt and pepper to taste.

Store in the refrigerator until required.

STEP 2. CRISP CURRANTS

INGREDIENTS
⅓ cup currants, roughly chopped

METHOD
Preheat the oven to 180°C and place the chopped currants on an oven tray. Cook in the oven for 6–10 minutes, then remove and let cool on the tray. Store in an airtight container until needed.

STEP 3. COOKING AND SERVING

INGREDIENTS
horseradish cauliflower purée
500 g smoked eel
1 bunch watercress or rocket
walnut oil
crisp currants
¼ cup toasted pine nuts

METHOD
Preheat the oven to 120°C. Place the purée in a small saucepan and warm over low heat, or microwave if you prefer. Now place the smoked eel in an ovenproof dish and heat for 5 minutes.

Divide the purée evenly between eight warm plates and then top each with one-eighth of the eel. Dress the watercress or rocket with a small amount of walnut oil and place a pile on top of the eel on each plate. Finally, garnish with the crisp currants, pine nuts and finish with another drizzle of the walnut oil.

STEVE'S WINE RECOMMENDATION

Kaituna Valley Pinot Noir
Typically, red wines are quite tannic and full bodied but Pinot Noir is an exception. It's usually more light-bodied with finer tannins so it doesn't dominate more delicate food items, including fish. Also, Pinot Noir has good acidity, which balances oily fishes, such as salmon and eel. The Kaituna Pinot Noir has plenty of complexity and interesting flavour notes that work well with our elegant and complex dish.

ACKNOWLEDGEMENTS

It's taken a mammoth effort by a bunch of people to get this book to print, and we would both like to take this opportunity to thank some special people who have helped in many ways to bring it all together.

First to our partners, Lizzie and Annette, who have supported (actually put up with) our continued absence from our homes, as we have juggled our lives and work commitments over the past two years. Your unwavering support and understanding has been immeasurable.

To the Logan Brown Restaurant team, especially Debs and Shaun, thank you for keeping this terrific restaurant of ours running like clockwork and giving us the chance to pursue not only *Hunger for the Wild* but all the other opportunities that have presented themselves along the way. Without your loyalty, constant hard graft and talents, we'd still be peeling onions or polishing glasses.

We also want to thank Gary Stewart of Ocean Design, who volunteered his time and work from the outset to give this book the unique look and feel that's before you. We love working with Ocean and are continually blown away by their extraordinary abilities to take our visions and turn them into a reality.

We would be lying to say we were the only authors of this book. Catherine Cordwell has had the unenviable job of co-writing this masterpiece. Her patience and calming attitude always at the forefront, and having to deal with us on a daily basis can't be underestimated! Writing into the wee hours of most nights, Catherine still managed to meet every deadline, as well as running Zest Food Tours and getting the kids off to school!

Our thanks also go to the exceptionally brilliant team at Fisheye Films. Pete Young (Producer/Cameraman) has been instrumental from the beginning, getting the whole *Hunger for the Wild* project off the ground. Pete sets high standards, and this, coupled with his natural talent, made this experience unique and challenging, and always a heap of fun. Tracy Roe's wonderful research and organisation set the foundation for a successful television series; all ably supported by the hard work of the rest of the crew: Gaylene, Sam, Veronica, Beth, Richard and Kendo. Pete and Tracy have also been instrumental in editing our book drafts.

Thanks to TVNZ for backing us and funding the series, particularly our commissioning editor Tony Manson.

Thanks also to Jenny Hellen and the team at Random House for all their hard work bringing this book to publication.

Lastly to all our new friends and acquaintances that we've met over this incredible country of ours. Thank you for sharing your worlds, your hunting and gathering spots, your history, your yarns, your kitchens and campfires. We feel very honoured to have been in the company of you all and we are proud to be 'Kiwis' and call New Zealand home.

Al Brown and Steve Logan, Wellington, September 2007

SOURCES

The following sources of information used to research this book provide more details on some of the information included in *Hunger for the Wild*. We would like to acknowledge these sources as well as thanking all those who have shared information with us for the book.

Crayfish on the rugged West Coast
Ministry of Fisheries — www.fish.govt.nz
NIWA Science — www.niwascience.co.nz
Seafood Industry Council — www.seafood.co.nz
Pickering, Mark, *The Southern Journey: a history of the travelling routes along the coast of Westland*, Christchurch, 1993.

Wild pigs up the Whanganui River
Wades Landing Outdoors Whanganui river journeys —
    www.whanganui.co.nz
www.wanganui.com
Te Ara — The Encyclopaedia of New Zealand — www.teara.govt.nz
National Library — http://teaohou.natlib.govt.nz

Whitebaiting on the Mokihinui River
Buller Community Development — www.westcoast.org.nz
Department of Conservation — www.doc.govt.nz
Hawes, Carolyn, *Great Expectations: the colonisation of the Buller*, Cadsonbury Publications, Christchurch, 2004
Pickering, Mark, *The Southern Journey: a history of the travelling routes along the coast of Westland*, Christchurch, 1993
Reed, A.W., *A Dictionary of Maori Place Names*, A.H. & A.W. Reed, Wellington, 1961

Wild rabbits in Central Otago
Central Otago District Council — www.codc.govt.nz
Cromwell and Districts Promotions Group — www.cromwell.org.nz
New Zealand Historic Places Trust — www.historic.org.nz
Otago Goldfields Heritage Trust — www.nzsouth.co.nz/goldfields
The Central Otago Wine Cellar — www.otagowine.com
Tourism Central Otago — www.centralotagonz.com
Rabbits — http://library.christchurch.org.nz
Titus, Paul, 'Chinese Heritage Given Boost', *Heritage*, New Zealand Historic Places Trust, Wellington, Spring 2003

Paua on the Wairarapa Coast
Castlepoint – www.castlepoint.co.nz
Go Wairarapa – www.wairarapanz.com

204 HUNGER FOR THE WILD

Masterton District Council — www.mstn.govt.nz
Paua Industry Council — www.paua.org.nz
Te Ara — The Encyclopedia of New Zealand – www.teara.govt.nz
Paua —
   https://www.iserve.co.nz/users/techs/pauashell.co.nz/htdocs/about-paua/

Pheasants in Rotorua
Destination Rotorua — www.rotoruanz.com
Fish and Game New Zealand — www.fishandgame.org.nz
Mokoia Island Restoration project —
   www.massey.ac.nz/%7Edarmstro/mokoia.htm
The Georgian Index — www.georgianindex.net

Flounder in Kawhia
Te Ara — The Encyclopedia of New Zealand — www.teara.govt.nz
Kawhia Tourism — www.kingcountry.co.nz
Oliver, Steven, 'Te Rauparaha, ?–1849', *Dictionary of New Zealand Biography*, www.dnzb.govt.nz

Paddle Crabs on the Kapiti Coast
Grays Underwater Site — www.geocities.com/wenraylm/crabtypes.html
Kapiti Coast District Council: http:www.kapiticoast.govt.nz, which was compiled with the help of historian Anthony Dreaver

Marlborough Scallops
Marlborough Online — www.marlboroughonline.co.nz
Ministry of Fisheries — www.fish.govt.nz
Royal Forest and Bird Protection Society — www.forestandbird.org.nz
Te Ara — The Encyclopedia of New Zealand — www.teara.govt.nz
Buick, Lindsay, *Old Marlborough*, Capper Press, Christchurch, 1976
Crabb, Peter, 'The Most Dangerous Animal in the Sea', *Viva Aqua*, November 2003, http://www.nzunderwater.org.nz
Maddock, Shirley, *A Pictorial History of New Zealand*, Heinemann Reed, Auckland, 1988
Wilson, John E., *AA Historic Places of New Zealand*, Hodder and Stoughton, Auckland, 1990

Eels on Banks Peninsula
Banks Peninsula Tourism — www.bankspeninsula.info
Horseradish — http://en.wikipedia.org/wiki/Horseradish
Te Ara — The Encyclopedia of New Zealand — www.teara.govt.nz
Our thanks to Don Jellyman at NIWA for checking our eel facts

IMAGE CREDITS

Peter Drury: 124–125

Kieran Scott: 11, 23, 25 (crayfish), 31, 43, 51, 58, 63, 83, 58 (rabbit), 101, 102 (paua), 121, 122, 123, 129, 140, 147, 161, 163 (crab), 179, 197

Rob Suisted/Naturepic: 66–67, 86–87, 104–105, 144–145, 164–165, 182–183

All other photographs taken by Peter Young, Tracy Roe and Sam Meehan

Maps by Holly Roach

INDEX OF RECIPES

pheasant
  leg confit 119
  pan seared breast with confit leg,
  Jerusalem artichoke puree and
  truffle oil 119
pipis in white wine 141
Puspa's crab curry 153

quarter pounder Mokihinui style 50

rabbit
  Eileen Scott's crumbed rabbit 72
  seared wild rabbit fillets with
  honey mustard vinaigrette 81
  wild rabbit and thyme stew with
  kumara fondant 82

sautéed flounder with fresh pipis in
  white wine, herbs and garlic 141
sautéed whitebait with fresh
  asparagus and beurre blanc sauce
  62

seared scallops with fresh corn and
  capsicum salsa 178
seared wild rabbit fillets with honey
  mustard vinaigrette 81
smoked eel pâté 191
smoked eel with horseradish
  cauliflower puree, crisp currants
  and pinenuts 196
sponge drops 58

tartare sauce 160

Waikanae crab cakes with tartare
  sauce 160
whitebait
  quarter pounder Mokihinui style
  50
  sautéed whitebait with fresh
  asparagus and beurre blanc sauce
  62
wild rabbit and thyme stew with
  kumara fondant 82